*I would like to dedicate this book to my mother Lily and my father Tom
who were so proud of their Irish heritage and my two brothers Séamus
and Hugh, who sadly passed away during the writing of this book.*

Text by Des Geraghty ©

Photography by Liam Blake ©

Foreword by Niall Crowley - Chief Executive Officer of the Equality Authority

Book and Jacket design by Brian Murphy

Published by Real Ireland Design.
Picture House 16/17 Bullford Business Park
Kilcoole, County Wicklow, Ireland

Tel: 00353 (1) 281 24 22
Fax: 00353 (1) 281 24 66
e-mail info@realireland.ie
web www.realireland.ie

© Picture Press.ie Ltd 2007

A CIP catalogue record for this book is available from the British Library.

ISBN 978-0-946887-15-6

This publication was printed and supported by Future Print, 25 Grange Parade, Baldoyle Industrial Estate.

Paper provided and supported by McNaughton Paper Ireland Ltd and Swan Paper.

The author of this book has made every effort to accredit all quotations used within.

40 Shades of Green

A wry look at what it means to be Irish

World BBQ competition, Limerick

Contents

Author's Note

This book owes its origin to a paper delivered by me, at the behest of my partner Rosheen Callender, SIPTU's National Equality Secretary, to the 2005 National Women's Forum entitled 'Organising Diversity'. Many people asked me for copies of that address and encouraged me to expand on the topic as they felt there was insufficient discussion taking place around the issues of identity, migration, racism and Irish attitudes to a more diverse and multi-cultural Ireland. Liam Blake was enthusiastic about capturing human images of the 'New Irish' and being part of this project and he introduced me to Real Ireland. Hence, our collaboration on this unique publication, which I hope you will enjoy.

I wish to thank all those who gave me help and assistance during the writing of this book, and who contributed ideas or information. I'm particularly indebted to Niall Crowley for his valuable introduction. I want to thank Rosheen for putting up with me, my daughters, Nóra and Eva, who gave great support and invaluable assistance with the mysteries of computer technology and the sourcing of material on the Internet, and Maeve and Alan for their warm encouragement. I'm grateful for Liam Blake's wonderful pictures and to all those who agreed to be photographed. Special thanks also to Mary Maher, Brian Murphy, Kathleen Flanagan, Joe Woods, Jane O' Hanlon, Roger Fox, Gerry Andrews and the Print Industry Forum, Future Print, Swan Paper and to poets Pearse Hutchinson and Vivienne Sullivan for their evocative poems.

Finally I want to thank all those who provided stories and expressed views and opinions on the wide-ranging subject matter of this book. I have tried to include where possible the experiences of many people with whom I have had dealings; trade union members, emigrants, migrants or just decent Irish people. For that, I thank them all. Ultimately however, the opinions expressed in the text are mine and mine alone and I take full responsibility for them.

A special thanks to the general officers and National Executive Council of SIPTU for their generous support and encouragement with this whole project.

Des Geraghty, Winter 2007

Foreword

In 'Forty Shades of Green', Des Geraghty deploys history, myth, literature and personal anecdote to unpick and examine the concept of 'Irishness'. He provides a timely and topical aid to assist the current debate on integration and cultural diversity in Irish society.

Moore Street, Dublin City, 'A long way now from Molly Malone'

The starting point for his examination is that 'The Irish' are 'not as easily packaged as some would like'. This of course makes a nonsense of responses to cultural diversity based on assimilation. How is it possible to demand of minority ethnic groups to assimilate with the identity of a majority that is both currently and historically made up of a diversity of identities and origins?

The Traveller community are highlighted by Des Geraghty as, 'the group that is perhaps the least integrated in Irish society'. This lack of integration is despite, or maybe even because of, decades of initiatives to assimilate the Traveller community into the majority ethnic community.

In 1963, a Government Commission on Itinerancy laid the foundations for this strategy of assimilation. It identified its central objective in the following terms:

'It is not considered that there is any alternative to a positive drive for housing itinerants if a permanent solution to the problem of itinerancy based on absorption and integration is to be achieved.'

By 1983, the language of assimilation had been softened. However the Report of the Travelling People Review Body in that year still suggested that an objective for education for Travellers was *'to give them freedom to make a real choice about their future way of life'*. The Review Body were clear as to what this choice should be when they recommended that *'newly wed couples who have to occupy caravans following their marriage should be considered extra sympathetically for housing to lessen the risks of regression to a travelling way of life.'*

The Task Force on the Travelling Community report in 1995 broke with this assimilationist approach in recommending *'that the distinct culture and identity of the Traveller community be recognised and taken into account'*. Despite this change, individual perception and institutional practices in relation to Travellers continue to be shaped by concepts of assimilation. More recently, political and popular debate has begun to pose assimilation as the way forward for the wider range of minority ethnic groups that are now part of Irish society.

However, Des Geraghty's work points to further difficulties, in that so many of the characteristics attributed to 'The Irish' are stereotypes based on false generalisations or are now dated and relegated to a distant past. He ends up having to pose the question −'So who are the real true blue Irish?'

In a context of new wealth and a rejection of traditional authority, Des Geraghty

Young school children

suggests 'there is evidence now of a genuine search by more concerned people for shared values of citizenship which could underline good public standards, a more meaningful Irish identity, in a more complex world.' A society in search of new values provides a context that is the antithesis of assimilation but that is promising for a more positive integration based on equality and mutual respect.

Integration and the emergence of an integrated society involves changes for both minorities and majorities. Integration needs to be based on a concept of Irishness that in the words of Mary Robinson, quoted by Des Geraghty, 'reaches out to everyone on this island'. An integrated society requires a value base that prizes equality, celebrates diversity and leaves no room for discrimination and exploitation. The search for a new and shared value base for Irish society provides an opportunity to ensure that all ethnic groups shape this value base.

It is important that this integrated society is not developed solely on the basis of a concern for diversity in cultural or ethnic terms. It is diminishing and unhelpful to impose singular identities on people. It is necessary to recognise and respond to the diversity of identities we all hold – ethnic and gender, disability, age, sexual, religious and others.

Des Geraghty highlights that 'much more will have to be done if our society is to facilitate a truly egalitarian order that rejects exploitation while genuinely accepting diversity and equality.' An integrated society will not emerge only on the basis of individual change within minorities and the majority group. It also requires institutional change. It needs all institutions and organisations to adapt how they conduct their business to better promote equality, ensure non-discrimination and adapt to diversity, including cultural diversity, among their employees, clients and customers. It needs institutions and organisations with a remit and resources to underpin a rights based approach to integration based on equality, diversity and non-discrimination.

Des Geraghty holds a long and proud tradition of work for a more egalitarian society. He continues that tradition in Forty Shades of Green with both humour and insight.

Niall Crowley

Niall Crowley is Chief Executive Officer of the Equality Authority and author of 'An Ambition for Equality' (Irish Academic Press).

Forty Shades of Green

Over the years there have been many less than complimentary assessments of the entity called 'Ireland' and even crude caricatures intended to neatly label 'the *Irish*'. These attempts are inclined to be glib generalisations that rarely do justice to the subject, or worse still end up as insulting characterisations. We 'the Irish' are a far more complicated lot, not as easily packaged as some would like. Yet most of us do retain a pride in our 'Irishness', however that is defined, and wish to retain our own sense of identity in the rapidly changing world we now inhabit.

While I hope we have left far behind the era of Mr Punch and the barbaric cartoon depictions, or indeed the 'pig in parlour' type pubs, or the Paddy Irishman jokes once so popular in Britain, at home we do have some residual self-image problems to address. Understandably our long association with drink, fighting or extreme nationalism has tended to define us in many quarters, but we have many other associations more worthy of remembrance. We do suffer the consequences of a long folk memory, however faulty that may be, but we have also demonstrated a great capacity to live for the day and hope for tomorrow. One description that has always had a ring of truth in it for me defines us as *'controlling ourselves manfully during the famine but losing our heads at the feast'*. Of course Oscar Wilde put it another way, *'Moderation is a fatal thing, Lady Hunstanton. Nothing succeeds like excess.'*

Brendan Behan, no stranger to feast or famine, made this non-PC remark, as he was prone to do, on our national psyche: *'Most people have a nationality, but the Irish and the Jews have a psychosis'*. James Joyce made the most unflattering comment that Ireland was *'the old sow that eats her farrow'*, yet in a more poetic mood, wrote; *'O Ireland my first and only love, where Christ and Caesar are hand in glove.'*

Of course all these generalisations fail to do justice to that diverse and self-confident group of people who now choose to define

Making a Malaysian contribution, Grafton Street, Dublin

11

themselves as part of the Irish nation. Making sense now of the various new Irish tribal groupings requires an appreciation not only of the people of the Republic but also the 'separated' brethren of Northern Ireland, both unionist and nationalist, and the approximately 80 million other people who now constitute that wider far-flung 'Irish diaspora' located in many distant parts of the globe.

President Mary Robinson made this the theme of her Presidency and spoke to the joint houses of the Oireachtas in her inaugural speech about the importance of this concept; *'Our relation with the Diaspora beyond our shores is one which can instruct our society in the value of diversity, tolerance and fair-mindedness.'* She also pointed out that *'Irishness as a concept seems to me at its strongest when it reaches out to everyone on this island and shows itself capable of honouring and listening to those whose sense of identity and whose cultural values may be more British than Irish'.* Lest we should ever forget the importance of the emigrant Irish, she reminded us of the truth of that insightful line from Evan Boland's poem, 'The Emigrant Irish', *'like oil lamps we put them out the back, of our houses, of our minds'.*

Much earlier, the Lord Mayor of Dublin Robert Briscoe, the first Jewish mayor of the city, referred to the phenomenon of the dispersed Irish when some US dignitaries visited the city, *'We welcome you in the name of 28 million inhabitants, 23 million of whom are in the United States.'* His estimate may now be considered somewhat conservative when you include all those who consider themselves to be Irish in other jurisdictions, however tenuous their claim to that description may be.

More and More Irish…

Now the arrival of the 'New Irish', hundreds of thousands from all continents, has added a fresh and sometimes exotic ingredient into the Irish mix. When you consider that the entire island population isn't much more than five million and approximately eighty million people proclaim their Irish identity, it's difficult not to conclude that we should accept henceforth that being Irish is far more to do with a state of mind than a state of place. Conor Cruise O'Brien, writing in the New Statesman, expressed the view that *'Irishness is not primarily a question of birth, blood or language; it is the condition of being involved in the Irish situation, and usually being mauled by it.'*

On the island, the 2006 census tells us that between 2002 and 2006 the population of foreign nationals over fifteen almost doubled, soaring from 190,000 to 367,000. That constitutes approximately one in nine of the adult population of the Republic. Foreign-born nationals account for 13 per cent of the population

Brazillians making merry in Gort, Co. Galway

of County Dublin and 10.7 per cent of County Galway, and have a much larger presence in some smaller towns. The meat industry in Gort first attracted skilled Brazilian workers in the 1990s; now 40 per cent of Gort's population is foreign-born, four out of five of them Brazilians. More than a third of residents in Ballyhaunis are foreign-born, with most from Eastern Europe; and if Paddy Reilly ever does heed the command of the song and come back to Ballyjamesduff, he'll find more than one-fourth of the locals are newcomers.

Most of these new arrivals are young. The census tells us that more than 60 per cent of those who came to Ireland in the year before April 2006 were single and in their twenties. Most have joined the active labour force and are contributing significantly to our economy. Many have also brought families seeking education and training or health and social services but are often later engaged in trade, commerce and job creation. Many are understandably looking for a better life for themselves and their families, and our expanding economy, with its need for more labour, has served as the main attraction. We also have an unknown number of undocumented migrants who tend to be the most vulnerable and most exposed to exploitation. There is also always the fear that if we were to experience a serious economic downturn many of these migrants would likely have to seek employment in pastures new.

But surveys suggest that at least half have a desire to stay on a medium to long-term basis. That makes them 'involved in the Irish situation' or opting to be part of this society by choice. Of course they will have all their own languages, beliefs and customs, not to mention colours or racial characteristics, but their option for remaining here makes them new members of our extended family and as such, a new part of what we now are. Inevitably a substantial number will remain here and share the future with us however it develops. It's already happening, as indicated by yet another interesting insight from the census into the way we are changing, the recorded increase in mixed nationality families from 70,721 in 2002 to 95,636 in 2006.

An example of the extent of the new diversity within the Irish population is illustrated by a recent review of services in FÁS, which discovered that on the 8th November 2006 half the visitors to FÁS offices were non-Irish nationals and that in total, 94 different nationalities were represented. It is estimated that there are now more than 200 different languages spoken regularly in Ireland though some are far more significant than others. Language is now a serious issue requiring our attention. We have certainly come a long way from the time when Brendan Behan could validly quip *'we have two languages in this country and both of them are a kind of foreign'*. There is no doubt that language is very often at the heart of people's identity. The Gaelic language has in the past been an important factor in determining our identity as a people but now both English and Irish may have a crucial role to play in defining who we will be in tomorrow's world.

The term 'Celtic Tiger' itself is a brand image of the recent economic reality, but it is hardly a sufficient identity label for proud people weaned on a strong sense of community, nor is it the embodiment of that 'terrible beauty' born in the imagination of the poet WB Yeats after the 1916 Rebellion. Or is our inheritance to be dominated by that earlier imagery of September 1913, when Yeats proclaimed that romantic Ireland was 'dead and gone'?

'What need you, being come to sense,
But fumble in a greasy till,
And add the halfpence to the pence,
And prayer to shivering prayer until
You have dried the marrow from the bone'

Amelia Stein, siúl eile

There is no doubt that there are a lot more of us now living on this island and all the evidence supports the view that that our population growth is likely to continue, irrespective of what might happen to the 'Celtic Tiger' economy. Those who stay will become the New Irish, or More Irish in time. The general populace is certainly looking a lot better, younger, brighter, more dynamic and self-confident. We are also more colourful and diverse, more productive, more optimistic, if somewhat more sceptical, about the authority or even the veracity of many of our once unquestionable institutions of church and state. There are few absolute certainties now, but people are generally better informed and better educated. They are certainly less subservient than previous generations. We are undergoing a 'sea change' but can we make of it something 'rich and rare'?

We are undoubtedly richer and more ambitious, but we increasingly display many of the more vulgar characteristics of the new rich as well. We have yet to come to terms with our recent material wealth and we have a lot more to do about genuine social solidarity, like paying our taxes, or ensuring universal access to high quality public services. Inequality and disadvantage still stand shoulder to shoulder with opportunity and success. Our traditional love affair with alcohol is rapidly being augmented with a potentially more lethal flirtation with newer addictions such as 'recreational' drugs, giving way to increased criminality and a harder drug culture.

Authority also used to be very simple in 'holy catholic Ireland'. Church and State operated in such a warm embrace that the individual citizen could be easily ignored. The awesome authority of both on issues of morality or behaviour allowed little room for public dissent. This was so pervasive that government departments often unquestioningly funded schools, hospitals, voluntary bodies and charitable institutions controlled by the churches, mainly catholic, with the minimum of accountability or supervision. The state abdicated its statutory responsibilities in many spheres and facilitated many abuses only recently acknowledged by both church and state. New legislation on weighty matters such as marriage, divorce, contraception, and school management, parental involvement in schools, corporal punishment or health research would never have been contemplated in the past by the State authorities without prior church approval.

Politics was in turn confined to a limited public sphere, while morality or ethics were very narrowly defined in religious terms alone. There was an unhealthy preoccupation of a celibate clergy with the sexual morality of others, along with a virtual disregard for the often blatantly immoral or unethical behaviour by 'good catholics' in many institutions. Politicians ran scared of clerical disapproval yet often tolerated low standards in other spheres of public life. During the early decades of the new state, censorship was extensive and severe because conservative churchman exercised enormous influence in most areas of Irish life. Many of our noteworthy writers were either banned or banished, while others chose a self-imposed exile as a personal statement of dissent from a very repressive society. Unfortunately, Ulster Unionists were able to make great political capital out of the perceived clerical 'Rome Rule' in the Republic over many decades following the partition of the country. One exile from that period, a personal friend of mine who left Ireland to live and write in England, recently described himself as 'growing up in Ireland in the era of the Taliban'.

An exasperated Dr Noel Browne TD, a veteran campaigner for reformed health

Liam O'flaherty, Man of Aran

services and welfare delivery, stated in 1971: *'No one can seriously doubt that the Catholic Church has behaved to all our political parties in an identical way as the Orange Order in its control of the Unionist Party in the North – a sectarian and bigoted politically conservative pressure group.'* The division of the country into a largely Protestant Northern entity and an overwhelmingly Catholic southern state did create the circumstances for sectarian political dominance in both jurisdictions.

In spite of the power politics of the churches, it is also true that many local clergy and religious orders of all denominations have worked and continue to work with their communities to enrich their lives in a variety of ways. Many of these true Christians have sought to overcome the enmities of the past and build a more tolerant, caring and peaceful society north and south. Their values are not dictated by personal gain or narrow sectarian interests but by a truly Christian ethic based on the belief that we should 'love our neighbour for the love of God'.

Now we like to believe that all the narrow sectarian dominance has 'changed utterly' and we have citizens who are more aware of their rights and no longer

accept unquestioned 'morality' policing by the leaders of church or state. We have moved beyond the notion that in Ireland there were only two classes: 'Catholics and Protestants on horseback'. Now we have a fair share of Catholics on horseback and a very broad collection of 'others' that could hardly be described simply as 'Protestants'. We now live in a more complex society with all the uncertainties that that entails but have not yet defined clear moral and ethical values for ourselves, which could help in developing a more inclusive society or become the accepted norms for good democratic governance in a pluralist society.

Big Jim Larkin

There is plainly a serious ambiguity about what now constitutes public morality in Ireland. The various tribunals have exposed many misdemeanours and malpractices in public bodies and the political system, which has yet to be exorcised fully. The public reactions to these have been mixed and sometimes bizarre in the extreme. But when I remember the theme of 'The Playboy of the Western World' by John Millington Synge, which gave dramatic expression to this syndrome, of the community in awe of 'the man who murdered his father', I am less surprised.

There is clearly a greater need for more openness and accountability in both public and private institutions. Yet there is also evidence now of a genuine search by more concerned people for shared values of citizenship, which could underline good public standards and a more meaningful Irish identity in a more complex world. In common with many other societies we face the challenge of enormous change, of a new multiculturalism and multilingualism as well as greatly changed concepts of how to define family, community or good citizenship.

Unfortunately, many of these changes are also coming as part of a society increasingly dominated by a new neo-liberal globalisation process and an insatiable appetite for more and more wealth, with all the questionable values this generates. There is also the Thatcherite doctrine to contend with, that there is now no such thing as society, a concept easily embraced by many of those who want to take all and give little back to their community.

Many of the changes in our world are also being driven by major technological advances and new forms of communication based on these technologies. Some of these technologies while supposedly increasing communication can also increase personal isolation and actually reduce real human contact and relationships. The control and shape of these technologies is all too often dictated by the requirements of major trans-national corporations or media tycoons who are fighting ruthlessly for dominance in an intensely competitive global economy. Yet the people part of that 'Globalisation' is still far from being resolved. The ground rules are ill defined and the much-hyped benefits are often very unevenly spread. While the technology changes rapidly we would do well to remember Edmund Burke's view that 'the march of the human mind is slow'. In many parts of the globe there are serious conflicts emerging between the value system of these exclusively market driven developments and the needs of societies to protect their own culture, values and a more people centred approach to living.

Who are the 'Real' Irish People?

'Ireland without its people means nothing to me'
James Connolly, Irish labour leader, executed after 1916 Easter Rising.

So who the hell are the Irish people now? How do we see ourselves and what is it that binds us together as a community? How can we address the future as a truly secure people, however diverse our origins, within an enlarged European Union, within a more competitive global world?

Can we cope comfortably with the waves of new arrivals on our shores and embrace their many different cultures? Can we achieve a meaningful inter-culturalism that works? Will we be able to combine our acute sense of history with a forward-looking approach to the new world order? Have we truly achieved the self-confidence necessary to develop a suitable set of values to define our Irishness in the modern world, while retaining those values which made us proud to be Irish in the past? Has our Gaelic language and culture got a role to play in the emerging Ireland? Is there space for people of all religions or none? Can we overcome the problems associated with living within the suffocating cultural space of Anglo-American influence with a shared English language and such overwhelming economic, social and political ties with both countries?

It could be argued that the real achievement of our recent economic success is that this generation has a real opportunity, perhaps for the first time, to develop a more self-confident sense of community defined by us, in our own terms. That represents a radical departure from our traditionally negative inward looking, or at times self-pitying or isolationist, approach to Irish identity. This was the more negative and defensive approach, which was more of an assertion that 'we are certainly not British,' even if we do speak their language. Of course we did play a major part in reshaping that language to our liking and making good use of it in our own inimitable way. Now it is evident that we can also live with many other languages and perhaps in the process even belatedly recognise the true value of our own.

I have often felt that the core of the identity problem in Northern Ireland is that many people of broadly similar backgrounds and history have too often sought to use symbols such as flags, churches or marches to demonstrate their differences, thereby perpetuating a form of negative identity, based on what they are not rather than what they are. That insecurity about identity sustains fear and fuels inter-communal tension, which then finds expression in sectarian hatred or violence. WR Ingle, Dean of Saint Pauls, in 'The Perpetual Pessimist' described, *'a nation as a society united by a delusion about ancestry and a common hatred of its neighbours'*. However that analysis pre dates the creation of the European Union.

Demonstrating that form of negative identity in politics and community relations has carried with it all the undesirable consequences that northern

A nation divided

Irish people have experienced over generations. Jonathon Swift put it in religious terms when he pointed out that *'we have just enough religion to make us hate, but not enough to make us love one another'*. There is much historic experience supporting the view that nationalist or tribal extremism of different varieties is rooted in power struggles and nurtured by fear, ignorance and insecurity. The fear is often associated with deep resentment against some 'threatening group' of outsiders or at times insiders who appear different. When we feel our own identity devalued or under threat we instinctively react defensively. This is a lesson that appears to have been missed by many world leaders and particularly by those who have, by their ill chosen words, demonised whole segments of society, indeed whole religions and nationalities. Unfortunately, unscrupulous politicians have often exaggerated a perceived racial or religious threat to perpetuate their own influence without reference to the consequences of their bigotry.

By way of contrast, it is evident that people with a clear sense of their own identity and worth have a real security about themselves and can live comfortably with diversity. Good economic and social planning can also play a major role and can create the positive environment for building that sense of security. It should be acknowledged however that we that have a lot of work to do, north and south, to cultivate more positive attitudes about the new diversity in our population and to begin to discuss more openly the changes needed to facilitate a healthy form of integration. As there is no serious external threat from our neighbours we should now be able to respond more generously to others of a different colour, creed or national identity in our midst.

Where do we Come From? – Out of the Celtic Twilight...

Sometimes we are still referred to as a Celtic country, in recognition of our rich Celtic heritage of arts and crafts, our ancient Gaelic language and culture and of course, our traditional music and song – not to mention our insatiable appetite for sport and revelry on all occasions. Our museums are full of beautiful Celtic artefacts and we have many ancient monuments that serve as constant reminders of an ancient civilisation on this island. Whether the Celtic label is the appropriate one or not, we have a valuable heritage from a very ancient civilisation and much in our traditions to be proud of. Unfortunately, the JCBs and the bulldozers of the get rich quick brigade have made a 'good job' of obliterating and destroying many of the remnants of that civilisation but some continue to survive, in spite of these philistines.

Giraldus Cambrensis (1147-1223), an early visitor to our shores, remarked on our musical skill; *'In the cultivation of instrumental music I consider the proficiency of this people to be worthy of commendation; and in this their skill is beyond all comparison, beyond that of any nation I have ever seen.'* That skill managed to survive to the present day and was often the only inheritance that poor emigrants had to pass on to the generations who came after them. Francis O'Neill (1848 -1936), who left Tralibane in Cork as a boy and became the Chicago Chief of Police in 1901, recognised the importance of that heritage and spent a lifetime collecting Irish tunes, trying to preserve the music for future generations. The Ulster poet of Dissenter stock, John Hewitt, recognised the power of that seductive musical heritage when he wrote,

'Among us, some, beguiled by their sad music,
make common cause with the natives,
in their hearts hoping to win a truce when the tribes assert
Their ancient right and take what once was theirs.'

Whether real or imagined, some characteristics considered to be Celtic continue to survive, but today could be more rightly described simply as a culture shared with Scots, Bretons, and Galicians, to be found also in places such as South Boston, Chicago, or Newfoundland. I'm also conscious that recent research utilising that new tool of archaeology, DNA, raises some serious questions about the origins of the 'Celtic' people and about many other treasured notions of race or national difference. However what matters most is the identity and shared values of the modern inhabitants of this island, some from our traditions, culture and shared history or from 'others' now wishing to 'be involved' with us, regardless of Conor Cruise O'Brien's, health warning about the serious risk of mauling.

Holy Catholic Ireland

On other occasions we have been referred to as a Catholic country (certainly true of the Republic) because of the large proportion of our population who define themselves as Catholics. We rarely define ourselves as Roman Catholics although others might. It was more normal in my youth to be described as Irish Catholics in a way that somehow suggested that we were the 'real' Catholics, not like those foreign and Protestant-type Catholics from France, Spain or Rome. While statistically, the Republic has always been over 90 per cent Catholic, that statistic has all too often been used to disguise a much greater variety of beliefs and outlooks among the populace. One such group, of whom there are more these days, would be those referred to jokingly as 'lapsed' or 'collapsed' Catholics. That term has been used to differentiate between cultural Catholics, which most of us are, and active practicing church-going Catholics. For example, when asked what religion he was, Brendan Behan described himself as a 'daylight atheist' in an Irish answer to an Irish identity problem.

I remember being slightly bemused by American visitors from Chicago, referring to themselves as Irish Catholics until I learned that they got the full Irish Catholic treatment of my childhood too; no half measures, no meat on a Friday, compulsory Sunday Mass with regular guilt trips about sexuality; missioners threatening hell fire and damnation, indulgences, the family rosary, penance, stern parish priests, nuns and disciplinarian Christian brothers, with a regular exposure to chaste, sexless, Irish dancing lessons to complete the treatment.

One such Chicago visitor to my home described himself as a 'Daley' Democrat conjuring up the firm link between 'Daily' religious observance and support for the Chicago Democratic Party. That particular identity did not extend to either Polish or Italian Catholics, not to mention the Roman variety. It was a classic example of the Irish political sub-culture of thinly disguised tribalism finding a means of surviving in the great melting pot of America politics where religion and political loyalty were inextricable.

Pilgrims Progress

Similarly, I remember the disdainful view many Irish people of my acquaintance in London had for English Catholics and their perceived religious observance or lack of it, describing them as another peculiar kind of upper class Protestants. That mutual Irish Catholic/Protestant disdain is well described in the joke about the Dublin visitor to Belfast who announced 'I'll never come back here again. It's cold, wet and full of Protestants.' Which evoked a witty Belfast Protestant retort: 'Go to Hell then, it's hot and dry and full of Catholics.'

The Emerald Isle

For many years we were typecast as a green isle of bliss because of the traditional rural life style and laid-back approach to life. On the notion of pleasant green pastures, I'm afraid our very poor environmental record has compromised the image of the Emerald Isle, with the EU watchdogs constantly questioning our green credentials. Dominic Behan wrote the song 'Thank God We're Surrounded by Water', but one wag suggested that we should thank God that we're regularly showered by water, or we would all be poisoned by pollution. Of course the rural green natural beauty has been compromised also by bungalow blight and ugly construction and dumping practices. Our love of the land has given way to the love of bricks and mortar on over priced building sites with poor planning standards.

The once famous friendly character of rural Ireland has also been well and truly hammered by some widely reported farmer hostility to hill walkers and backpackers on 'their' mountains. I doubt if many of our patriot dead, particularly Wolfe Tone's 'large and respectable class, the people of no property' would have appreciated the extent to which private property rights have been defined to the virtual exclusion of any complimentary notion of the common good. To complete the picture, our opportunistic reputation for overcharging and often providing poor value for money has shattered any fanciful notions we once had about our genuine belief in a 'céad mile fáilte' for visitors or for our own hard pressed urban dwellers seeking some solace from frantic city life in the tranquillity of the countryside.

For me, none of the traditional depictions of our uniqueness were ever entirely valid. Yet thankfully, some valuable features of our cultural heritage have managed to survive. We are still capable of an outgoing warmth and friendliness that strangers recognise easily. We have generally retained a strong sense of community or even a tribal loyalty and often a genuine concern for people less fortunate than ourselves. Surprisingly, in some respects, our traditional love of sport, 'craic' and music continues to thrive in a multitude of forms, old and new, in both urban and rural areas. We have also managed, for better or worse, to preserve an almost instinctive identity with 'underdogs' irrespective of the rights and wrongs of their cause.

The national sports of Gaelic Football and Hurling continue to attract fierce local or even tribal loyalty in most areas of the country, although all sports, irrespective of their origins, appear to be thriving these days. The decision of the GAA to open

Noah's Ark

Croke Park, with all of its sacred history, to rugby and soccer was a major advance in that regard as it demonstrated finally that a more tolerant and outward looking sense of Irishness can live comfortably with a strong awareness of our own history and traditions. There are serious sectarian issues yet to be addressed by the GAA, particularly in Northern Ireland, but there is every reason to believe that they are being addressed and will eventually be resolved. Although curiously enough, in recent years it was the soccer supporters of 'Jack's Army' who did most to define a modern 'Irishness' on the international stage, demonstrating not just our genuine love of fun and games but also an ability to share a good natured national sportsmanship, in victory or defeat.

Then again, at the rate we have been building golf courses here, we may well have to reconsider what constitutes the national sport. As a youngster I played hurling with my friends, but one of my daughters took up cricket. She assures me that cricket was very popular here 100 years ago, often putting the standard of hurling to shame in certain places generally considered to be hurling strongholds, including Kilkenny, right up until World War 1.

Irish cricket experienced a huge surge in popularity recently when the Irish team displayed world-class skill in the Cricket World Cup 2007. Ireland's fast bowler, Boyd Rankin, astonished the world by dismissing three of Pakistan's best batsmen on St Patrick's Day and the team went on to win the match. The 22 year old was awarded the BBC Radio Foyle/Bank of Ireland Sports Personality of the Month Award for his performance. I'm not quite sure how cricket and hurling will co-exist here but it looks promising.

An fear is fearr, Aran Islander.

The Black Irish

'Ireland's traditional missionary role of proselytising has been largely replaced by charity and development work abroad. The approach to both is now generally more enlightened than when I first came to Ireland. I was horrified then to find school children still buying black babies'

Gretchen Fitzgerald (Fernandes) from Goa, India, 1992

The issue of colour often associated with racial prejudice has not always been a major problem in our society yet it is one that must be addressed. The number of coloured people in Ireland was once so small that they were scarcely noticed; yet colour has featured in our relations with other migrant groups in the US, Britain and further a-field. My earliest exposure to the notion of colour difference started with a near neighbour of distinctly dark features who worked for The South of Ireland Ashphelt Co. now known as SIAC. He was referred to as 'Blackie'. There were others referred to as 'Coalies', men who worked in the coal yards and found that carbolic soap couldn't restore the whiter than white complexion of their birthright. Individuals of the genuine coloured skin variety were few and far between, apart from medical students, hospital doctors or the rare stray British soldier.

The odd black, brown or yellow sailor might be spotted on the quays on occasions; a very rare coloured child of mixed parentage might appear in school, but in general we were pale white creatures with only the small touch of red, engendered by our sensitivity to sunshine. Black babies were far away in Africa, sufficiently distant to threaten nobody except the good nuns and priests involved in the missions. We never expected that one day they might come calling to see for themselves where the good priests and nuns came from.

Paul Robeson, the black American singer, was a great favourite in our house next only to John McCormack. We heard both on our record collection of old 78s, played regularly on the wind-up gramophone. Robeson's struggle for equality and human dignity was often discussed at home, while we listened to his deeply moving versions of Kevin Barry, Castle of Dromore, Lindy Lou, Joe Hill or Old Man River. We were also reasonably familiar with the Black and White Minstrels, not so PC these days, in particular Al Jolson, whose songs in the style of 'Way Down upon the Swanee River' were great family favourites. That was long before Elvis made black gospel music part of our pop culture or Ray Charles sought to 'take these chains from my heart and set me free'.

We were kept well informed by teachers and the clergy about the world of the 'Black Babies' in far off places, who required all our pennies and halfpennies for their salvation. I was personally very taken with the cause of Blessed Martin who actively adorned a large collection box in our schoolroom, nodding his black head as you inserted your small donation. I even adopted the name Martin for my Confirmation, in solidarity with this dark, saintly gentleman.

I believe my childhood dedication was suitably rewarded many years later when a Dublin employer in the haulage business refused to deduct union contributions from his employees. This was a time when the weekly collection of union dues from mobile and often casual drivers was a near impossible task. After some initial conflict with this hardheaded employer about industrial relations matters we developed a reasonable modicum of mutual respect. He continued to refuse to do the 'union's job' of collecting union dues but as a gesture of good will to me personally, he instructed the wages clerk to deposit the union contributions in the Blessed Martin collection box. This wooden box with the nodding black holy man on top was suitably nailed to the counter, and I was provided with the only key to the lock. When I subsequently collected the union money for the ITGWU, I was always guaranteed a friendly nod from my black soul mate.

Another story about those unfortunate Black Babies comes from a friend of mine who was walking down Ranelagh Road in Dublin on a fine Sunday morning. Crowds of black people in their Sunday best were crowding into a small Seventh-Day Adventist Church. There was a large Irish country gentleman glowering at this gathering making his disdain obvious to passers-by. 'Would you look at them? Would you look at them!' When asked by my friend what was wrong with them, he retorted 'Why did we bother sending all that money to the missionaries for the black babies when that's the kind of church they end up in?' This was obviously a clear case of 'better pagan than Protestant'.

An interesting if racially abusive term – 'Black Irish' – crops up frequently in our history abroad. It is associated with groups of Irish or their descendants exhibiting behaviour associated with a particular stereotype of the Irish. The most common references to this are associated with US and UK notices in boarding houses or employments stating: 'No Irish or Blacks need apply'. Historically the term 'Black Protestants' has been used as a term of abuse, particularly but not exclusively in Northern Ireland, but is not very commonly used in the Republic except where the folk memory of tyrannical Protestant landlords still remains strong.

According to some historians, the etymology of the term 'Black Irish' seems rooted in the events surrounding the Spanish Armada at the end of the 1500's, which landed thousands of shipwrecked Spanish sailors on the west coast. Hundreds of these dark swarthy strangers found a secret refuge with isolated Irish coastal communities. Their heritage is obvious in the prevalence of dark hair, dark eyes, dark skin and Mediterranean features still evident amongst the western populace.

Ghanain sisters

The Spanish Armada was instigated by Phillip 11 of Spain in 1588, in defence of the Catholic religion following the death of Mary Queen of Scots and in response to piracy by British ships against Spanish shipping in the English Channel en route to the trade ports of Holland.

In a very sad comment on human savagery and on 'man's inhumanity to man', James Hardiman in his 'History of the Town of Galway 1820', recorded that when hundreds of the ship wrecked Spanish and Portuguese sought refuge in the west of Ireland, the British authorities set out to have them rounded up and murdered;

'Sir Murrough O'Flaherty, William Burke, the Blind Abbott, and several of the principal inhabitants of Mayo and Iar-Connaught, came in and submitted, but were put under conditions to give hostages, disperse their forces, deliver up all the Spanish and Portuguese to whom they had given refuge. Sir William Fitz-William, while he remained in the town, caused several of the Spaniards delivered up on this occasion to be beheaded near St. Augustine's monastery on the hill, amidst the murmurs and lamentations of the people. Having wreaked vengeance on these unfortunate men, he departed for Dublin.'

Post-mortem

Another theory relates to the thousands of Irish slaves sent to the West Indies where they were intermingled with black African slaves. The prevalence of the Irish in that region led to the island of Montserrat being called the Emerald Isle of the Caribbean. It is perhaps worth remembering that many of the 'coffin ships' used to transport Irish famine victims to the New World had only recently been somewhat decommissioned as slave trader vessels. In short, the poor Irish often arrived in slave-like conditions to their destinations in the New World. The etymologist, Cassells, suggested that the term 'Black Irish' was used to describe a lower class, unsophisticated, perhaps unkempt Irish immigrant in the United States. In other cases in the West Indies, he identifies it with former slaves who adopted the name of a former Irish owner.

Black Slavery

'I am here then in order to avoid the scent of the blood hounds of America, and of spreading light on the subject of her slave system. There is nothing slavery dislikes half as much as the light. It is a gigantic system of inequity, that feeds and lives in darkness, and, like a tree with its roots turned to the sun, it perishes when exposed to the light.'
Frederick Douglass, escaped black slave leader, speaking in Cork, 14th October 1845, powerfully depicted in Donal O'Kelly's play, 'Arcadia'.

Given the persistence of colour prejudice in many countries, including Ireland, it is interesting to remember that 'colour prejudice' was not always a universal feature in our past. Many black anti-slavery campaigners sought support from the Irish. One of those was Olaudah Equiano as early as 1790. Equaino was a black Nigerian slave who bought his 'freedom' and wrote his own story in the book, 'The Interesting Narrative of the Life of Olaudah Equiano or Gustavus Vassa'. When the black abolitionist former slave, Frederick Douglass visited Ireland at the outbreak of the Famine in 1845, he paid a glowing tribute to his audiences in Ireland and to the Liberator Daniel O'Connell who was a noteworthy abolitionist during his political career.

Speaking in Cork after fleeing America to keep out of the clutches of his former slave owner he proclaimed: *'I never more than at present lacked words to express my feelings. The cordial and manly reception I have met with, the spirit of freedom that seems to animate the bosoms of the entire audience have filled my heart with feelings I am incapable of expressing. I stand before you in the most extraordinary position that one human being ever stood before his race – a slave.'*

He went on to tell his audience that Daniel O'Connell did much to abolish slavery:

'I feel grateful to him, for his voice has made American slavery shake at the centre – I am determined where ever I go, and whatever position I may fill, to speak with grateful emotions of Mr O'Connell's labours. I heard his denunciation of slavery, I heard my master curse him and therefore I loved him. In London, Mr O'Connell tore the mask of hypocrisy from the slave holders and branded them as the vilest of the vile, the most execrable of the execrable, for no man can put words together stronger than Mr O'Connell.'

He came to Dublin also where Richard Davis Webb agreed to publish the British edition of his autobiography Narrative of the Life of Frederick Douglass, an American Slave. 'Webb was a Quaker who edited The Anti-Slavery Advocate'.

Limerick BBQ

In a scathing attack on double standards, Douglass, who became a minister of the African Methodist Episcopal church, condemned the connection of religion and the white Christian churches:

'In America, Bibles and slave-holders go hand in hand. The Church and the slave prison stand together and while you hear the chanting of psalms in one, you hear the clanking of chains in the other. The man who wields the cowhide during the week, fills the pulpit

on Sunday – here we have robbery and religion united – devils dressed in angels' garments. The man who whipped me in the week used to attend to show me the way of life on the Sabbath.'

Anti-slavery activity was widespread in Ireland. In 1837 the Hibernian Anti-Slavery Society was founded in Dublin and thousands of Irish people supported a boycott of slave-grown sugar. It's also worth remembering that most Irish nationalists saw the direct parallel between the oppression of the Irish people and the barbaric treatment of black slaves, though surprisingly there are exceptions such as John Mitchell. Mitchell was a leading Young Irelander who was transported to Tasmania, 'Van Diemen's Land', for his part in the armed insurrection of 1848, yet he later supported the Confederacy and defended slavery in America, *'I consider Negro slavery here the best state of existence for the Negro and for his master'.* (1857 in the The Southern Citizen.)

In a recent book entitled Encounters- How Racism Came to Ireland, Bill Rolson and Michael Shannon argue convincingly that the Irish have had many encounters with black and coloured people over the centuries in many situations and in many parts of the world where they were often 'part of the forces colonising or subjugating the people of colour.' They point out the extensive involvement of Irish Catholics in the colonial service of the British Empire as soldiers and civil servants. For example in 1830 Irish men constituted 42% of the British army and in 1857 Irish universities provided 33% of Indian civil service recruits. They point out that; *'Throughout the British Empire, where there were military campaigns, defeated local forces, repression, massacre and racism, the chances are that Irish people were centrally involved in designing, administering or enforcing British rule- generals and rank and file soldiers, governors and clerks.'* Yet they also acknowledge that while there were many examples of mutual respect and solidarity between the Irish and the oppressed peoples, we can hardly deny our involvement in upholding racism and inequality in many distant lands.

Marcus Garvey, former secretary of the National Club of Jamaica, modelled his struggle for black people's rights on the Irish struggle. In 1919 he called his headquarters in New York 'Liberty Hall' in honour of James Connolly and sent a telegram to De Valera in 1920 stating: *'We believe Ireland should be free even as Africa shall be free for the Negroes of the world.'* He also called for a boycott of British ships in the U.S. in protest at the treatment of Terence Mac Swiney, the Lord Mayor of Cork who died on hunger strike in 1920.

In more recent times, a good friend of mine, the late Gretchen Fitzgerald (Fernandes), from Goa, India, wrote from a different perspective on the Irish in a pamphlet entitled 'Repulsing Racism': *'Racial prejudice is prejudice against people who look, speak, dress, or behave differently from 'us' because of their ethnic origins or culture. We are all guilty of racial prejudice, weather we are Indian, Irish or European. Such prejudice is often based on ignorance or fear, particularly when there is little contact between people of different nations or ethnic groups.'* She also pointed out that *'experiencing racism does not prevent one being racist oneself'*.

Gretchen drew particular attention to our deep-rooted racist attitudes and behaviour towards Travellers.

'The prejudice and discrimination against Travellers is similar to that practised by white people against black people. Travellers' skin colour does not protect them from racist thinking and behaviour, which is based on the ethnic and cultural differences between Travellers and 'settled' people. In some respects our anti-traveller prejudice is the most enduring and ingrained of our racial prejudices and, given our mutual antipathy, it may prove to be the most difficult to eradicate.'

The Fighting Irish

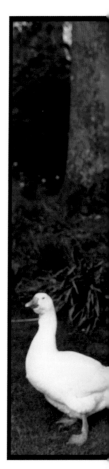

'For the great Gaels of Ireland
Are the men that God made mad,
For all their wars are merry,
And all their songs are sad'
GK Chesterton

Then there's the dictum that 'we fought every nation's battles but our own'. I was never completely sure about that, considering our apparent capacity for local wars or skirmishes with the historic enemy in virtually every generation, North or South of the border. But it is undoubtedly the case that we lost many, many of our young fighting men in other peoples' wars over the centuries. From the 'Wild Geese' (the Irish Chiefs who had supported the Jacobite cause and who emigrated in great numbers after the Treaty of Limerick 1691 which ended the Williamite war in Ireland) and for at least two centuries afterwards, we were certain to feature in every bun fight, in every generation, on virtually every continent, often on both sides of the argument.

The remarkable fact is that the majority of our fighting was done within the British Army, the army of the oppressor, even by ardent nationalists. Due to persistent unemployment and poverty over the centuries, the British military option was a convenient escape route for young Irish men. While we can all remember with pride the one thousand plus Volunteers and Citizen Army men who turned out in

1916 in Dublin, more than 70,000 Irish from north and south were reported dead, wounded or missing in Flanders as members of the British Army. Hundreds of thousands of young Irishmen fought in that dreadful war, many of them were there in support of Home Rule, but others were there because they were poor, unemployed or had no other prospects at home. In stark contrast, many Ulstermen were also there to prevent Home Rule and to defend their union with Britain.

There was always a brisk trade in cannon fodder among the lower orders of town and country, with a goodly supply of recruiting agents to capitalise on this lucrative trade. Landlords encouraged it to get rid of troublesome tenants, families established a tradition of military service over many generations, and the poor of the towns and cities were always prey to the recruiting sergeant. The local ascendancy also produced many career soldiers of the officer class, ensuring a ready supply of militia to put down rebellion in times of strife.

However, we never confined our fighting to the British military, and as a consequence the Irish appear in the history of many an army, often on both sides of the argument, with particularly poignancy during the American Civil War. While our involvement in the United States conflicts and those of the United Kingdom are generally well known we did not confine our fighting to those war fronts. Irish emigrants also featured prominently in the various conflicts of central and South America. William Brown is probably the best remembered Irishman in Argentina, where he is considered a national hero. Brown was born in Foxford in County Mayo in 1777 and died in Buenos Aires in 1857. He created the Argentine navy and led the armed forces of that country

Trinity professor

in the wars against Brazil and Spain. In the 19th and 20th centuries more than 50,000 Irish emigrants went to Argentina, while today there are 500,000 people of Irish ancestry or approximately 12.5% of the population of that country.

Another famous Argentinean who became an iconic figure and whose memory is still revered by poor and oppressed people in many parts of the world was Che Guevara the Cuban revolutionary and minister in Castro's Government, killed later near La Higuera in Bolivia. Guevara's grandmother was a Lynch and his father Ernesto Guevara Lynch said of him *'The first thing to note is that in my son's veins flowed the blood of the Irish rebels.'* Of course Guevara considered himself to

Saint Patrick's Day

be a Latin American revolutionary of Cuban and Argentine extraction, but was fully aware of his Irish ancestry. Irish Times journalist Arthur Quinlan interviewed Che in Shannon on a stopover to Prague on the 13th March 1965 and spoke to him about his Irish ancestry and his roots in Galway. Having adjourned with his friends to Hanratty's Hotel on Glentworth Street in Limerick, Che and his friends returned to the airport proudly sporting sprigs of shamrock.

The Irish influence in Argentina was not confined to fighting. 'The Southern Cross' Catholic newspaper founded in 1875 and continuing to print to this day, was founded by Dean Patricio Dillon, an Irish emigrant and a deputy for Buenos Aires. That paper also carries material in the Irish language to enable Irish-Argentineans to continue to keep in touch with their cultural heritage. Two Dublin-born brothers, Edward and Michae Mulhall published 'The Standard', allegedly the first daily English language newspaper in South America, while later the leader of Argentina from 1943 to 1946 was Edelmiro Julian Farrell whose paternal ancestry was Irish.

In Mexico there is an interesting episode in history when Mexican Texans known as the 'Batallón de San Patrico' sided with the Catholic Mexicans against the US army in the war of 1846-1848. There is a monument to the 'Los Patristas' in the fort of Churubusco. A Wexford man named William Lamport, known to the Mexicans as Guillen de Lampart, was the author of the first proclamation of independence. His statue stands today in the Crypt of Heroes beneath the column of Independence in Mexico City. Some have suggested that Lamport was the inspiration for Johnston McCulley's film character Zorro. Mexico has a large number of people of Irish ancestry among them the actor Anthony Quinn. Alvaro Obregón, reputedly O'Brien, was president of Mexico from 1920-24.

Many of the Wild Geese, expatriate soldiers and their families who initially went to Spain, ended up in South America and achieved prominence there. In the 1820's some of their descendants fought to liberate that continent. Bernardo O'Higgins was the first president of Chile. When Chilean troops occupied Lima in Peru in 1881 in the War of the Pacific, they were under the command of Patricio Lynch whose grandfather came from Ireland to Argentina and later to Chile.

The story of Irish involvement in the Venezuelan War of Independence is even more surprising given how little we now know about that important country, which is generating strong 'winds of change' in the region today. The British Legion, remembered each year for their part in the struggle for the liberation of Venezuela, under 'The Liberator' Simon Bolivar, were mainly Irish, with smaller numbers of English, Welsh and Scottish fighters. It began as the Irish Legion in 1812 under Bolivar and went on to play a major part in the famous and decisive battle of Carabobo on June 24th 1821, an event proudly commemorated in Venezuela each year.

One thousand Irish men of the Irish Legion landed on Margarita Island in 1819 and a further two thousand one hundred Irish soldiers joined their forces in the next few years. A further twelve thousand followed and supported Bolivar in his fight against Spanish colonialism. Bolivar's personal Aide-de-Campe was Daniel Florence O'Leary from Cork, (whose mother was from Belfast), who became his military and political strategist and rose to the rank of Brigadier General. His remains lie in a special place of honour with the remains of The Liberator himself in the National Pantheon in Caracas.

A sad aspect of that conflict was the fate of thousands of unfortunate Irish emigrant soldiers who travelled over four thousand five hundred miles to the shores of Venezuela to die in the harsh tropical sun, starving and diseased in flea infested shacks on the shores of Margarita Island. They succumbed to outbreaks of typhoid, dysentery and yellow fever. Morgan O'Connell, son of the Irish Liberator, Daniel O'Connell was one of the survivors who joined Bolivar in June 1820 and at the age of fifteen, becoming the Irish Legions youngest officer.

Thomas D'Arcy McGee, a prominent Young Irelander and author of the poem 'The Celts', is reputed to have been largely responsible for the vision behind the Confederation of the British North American colonies as the Dominion of Canada. He worked for 'The Nation', the newspaper of the Young Ireland movement, and was arrested and imprisoned because of his support for the 1848 revolutionary activities but escaped soon after to the United States. There he started a newspaper known as The 'Nation', and later The American Celt. He later moved to Montreal in Canada and won a seat in the Canadian Parliament. Ironically he became a supporter of the Canadian Confederation under British jurisdiction and speaking in the Canadian Parliament in 1860, he outlined his vision of a future Canada;

'I see in the not remote distance one great nationality, bound like the shield of Achilles, by the blue of the ocean. I see it quartered into many communities, each disposing of its own internal affairs, but all bound together by free institutions, free commerce...'

Russian grave digger

His support for a British Canada gave rise to his assassination by a reputed Fenian sympathiser, just after the creation of The Dominion of Canada and months before the celebration of the first anniversary of that event on 1st, July 1868.

The Irish were also prominent in Peru in the struggle against the Spanish under Colonel Francis Burdette O' Connell. He was Chief of Staff under General Antonio Jóse de Sucre and was responsible for the military strategy at the decisive Battle of Ayacucho. He went on with Sucre to liberate Upper Peru and helped to establish Bolivia as a separate independent nation. There he was promoted to General and lived out his life as a Bolivian farmer with a Bolivian wife and family. These disposed Irish emigrants were examples of the hundreds of thousands of Irish people who left their home country in search of a better life and so often found nothing but hardship and death from disease, or fighting in foreign wars thousands of miles from home.

'Well, it's by the hush, me boys, and sure that's to hold your noise
And listen to poor Paddy's sad narration.
I was by hunger pressed and in poverty distressed
So I took a thought I'd leave the Irish nation.
Here's you boys, now take my advice
To America I'll have yous not be comin'
There is nothin' here but wars where the murderin' cannons roar
And I wish I was at home in dear old Ireland.'
Paddy's Lamentation - traditional emigrant song.

It's difficult not to conclude that over the centuries of our peoples' attempted escape from poverty and oppression here, the poorest were frequently used as an expendable commodity in other peoples' conflicts. But then, poor people have always been considered expendable by their 'betters'. We certainly had a disproportionate and often disastrous involvement in other peoples' wars, although our experience as dispossessed migrants or 'economic refugees' is unfortunately not absolutely unique.

Bosnian mother

Chernoble child

In more recent times the most honourable involvement of the Irish in foreign wars was the Connolly Column in the Spanish Civil War 1936-39, where many Irish volunteered to oppose the Fascist take-over of Spain by General Franco as part of the International Brigade. Of course, to complete the picture, another group under General Owen O'Duffy, leader of the Irish Blueshirts, went to Spain to support their hero General Franco, although it is claimed that their involvement in fighting was more notional than real.

Of course many well-motivated Irish volunteers did join other foreign armies, particularly the British, American and Canadian and Australian forces to oppose Adolf Hitler and German Fascism during the 1939-1945 World War. We have in addition established an honourable Irish tradition of overseas peace-keeping in the service of the United Nations and have lost many soldiers in difficult and troubled parts of the world because of that international commitment.

My favourite comment about our historic addiction to fighting is that of the old woman who is reputed to have said: *'The Black and Tans are gone and the soldiers are gone, and the polis is going, so now our boys can get on with fighting in peace.'*

The Dirty Irish

'This is a filthy people, wallowing in vice. Of all people it is the least instructed in the rudiments of the faith.'
Cambrensis Giraldus, 12th century visitor to Ireland

Another form of identity is that less respectful one, 'the dirty Irish', a description used by some of our more insulting detractors in the past. Undoubtedly, the association of poverty, famine, disease and malnourished emigrants all contributed to the persistence of that image. That was also the depiction of the bold Giraldus in the 12th century who appreciated our musical ability but was far less complimentary about our cleanliness or our faith. A similar uncomplimentary sentiment about our standards of hygiene was expressed in a report in 1804, which stated that:

'the want of cleanliness, for which the lower orders of the Irish are in general distinguished, together with the inflammatory state of body created by the quantity of ardent spirits which they swallow, must make those diseases which are the scourge of such crimes, more violent in their symptoms than in other places.'

At the other extreme, there was the idea of 'the saintly Irish', probably a deliberately misleading rumour started by ourselves. No one has ever convinced me that this country was ever really an 'island of saints and scholars'. We had some scholars no doubt, but the saintly bit is more tenuous. Nor did we actually ever come very close to President Eamon De Valera's rural idyll of a people living in 'frugal comfort', in a land where:

'...fields and villages would be joyous with the sounds of industry, the rompings of sturdy children, the contests of athletic youths and the laughter of comely maidens; whose firesides would be forums for the wisdom of serene old age. It would, in a word, be the home of a people living a life that God desires that man should live'.

Quite a wonderful concept for a Celtic mystic or a poet, but hardly the stuff that real life is made of in Ireland or anywhere else. Yet, it was Dev's concept of an independent Irish Republic that shaped Irish political culture for decades after the foundation of the Free State in 1921. It was not until the election of Seán Lemass as Taoiseach in 1959 and the National Development Programmes of T.K. Whitaker (Secretary of the Dept. of Finance and later, Governor of the Central Bank 1969-1776), that we began to carve out an identity which sought to combine patriotism with economic and social development of a more outward looking variety.

Eoin MacNeill, the leader of the Irish Volunteers in the era of the 'Celtic Twilight' was once forced in a somewhat exasperated mood to state: *'We must remember that what we call our country is not a poetical abstraction, as some of us are sometimes apt to imagine… There is no such person as Cáitlín Ní Ullacháin or Róisín Dubh or the Sean Bhean Bocht who is calling us to serve her. What we call our country is a concrete and visible reality'.*

None of these traditional images was ever wholly accurate. Nor could they ever be so, when seeking to describe a whole society of diverse individuals living on this island. Even less accurately do they describe the very much more diverse Irish diaspora scattered across the five continents, but still clinging to an Irish identity. The tongue-in-cheek chauvinism of the Irish Diaspora was best illustrated for me on a New York T-shirt on St Patrick's Day, with the slogan: *'There are only two types in the world, Irish and those who wish they were.'* When you saw the multitudes sporting the green on that occasion you might even be tempted to believe our own propaganda, especially after a few pints of Guinness and a green, cream whiskey chaser.

Of course many of the classical depictions of us are as phoney as 'Paddy whack' or the plastic leprechauns with Déanta sa tSeapáin (made in Japan) stamped on the back in the tourist shops of Kerry and the West of Ireland. The Irish theme pub is another recent creation of the vivid Irish imagination, more akin to the New York bars than any to be found in Ireland. The Harp and the Shamrock were adopted as marketable symbols of Irishness and served us well as national brands in the sale of Irish goods and services over many decades when other symbols of our true identity were in short supply.

The ghoulish cartoons of Mr Punch, so typical of the British

Faces in the crowd

Dutch designer

establishment's prejudicial view of the Irish in the 19th century, were another example of unfair generalisation. The anti-Irish views of that particular journal, such as the following, would now certainly be condemned as inciting race hatred:

'A creature manifestly between the Gorilla and the Negro is to be met with in some of the lowest districts of London and Liverpool by adventurous explorers. It comes from Ireland, whence it has contrived to migrate; it belongs in fact to a tribe of Irish savages; the lowest species of the Irish Yahoo. When conversing with its kind it talks a sort of gibberish. It is moreover, a climbing animal, and may sometimes be seen ascending a ladder with a hod of bricks. The Irish Yahoo generally confines itself within the limits of its own colony, except when it goes out of them to get its living. Sometimes, however, it sallies forth in states of excitement, and attacks civilized human beings that have provoked its fury. The somewhat superior ability of the Irish Yahoo to utter articulate sounds, may suffice to prove that it is a development, and not, as some imagine, a degeneration of the Gorilla.'

The Celts

'Long, long ago beyond the misty space of twice a thousand years,
In Erin old there dwelt a mighty race, taller than Roman spears'
From 'The Celts', by Thomas D'Arcy McGee

If the ancient mythology about the Celts is correct, they were preceded by Milesians, Tuath Dé Danann, Fir Bolgs and other exotic tribes seeking to make a homeland on this island before they were overtaken by other new arrivals. No doubt the earlier tribes left many of their number here after having to come to terms with the conquest of the newcomers.

The Celts were a somewhat amorphous lot. Their history is deeply obscured by retelling of old legends, storytelling suitably embroidered with mythology, colourful language and exaggeration. When our people were at their lowest ebb, after so many defeats they could take courage and inspiration from the exploits of their supposed once mighty and unconquered ancestors.

What we call the Celts would appear now to have been made up of diverse tribal groups of somewhat uncertain origin. They did not describe themselves as 'Celts' nor did they arrive as a single entity. They appear to have come in a succession of waves conquering those who came before and absorbing them into the new order as they gained dominance.

There is some dispute among scholars about their origins, some suggesting middle Europe, although recent evidence would tend to favour the Atlantic sea routes, from the Mediterranean region via Spain, Brittany, Cornwall. It appears that the Gael were the last of those Celtic arrivals, conquering the whole of the country and dominating the island for almost one thousand years. One of the most distinguishing features of this group was the Gaelic language, which has survived in Ireland, in a variety of forms, up to the present day.

The Romans, significantly, never did us the favour of conquering the island. After having a difficult time suppressing the tribal inhabitants of Britain they probably had little appetite for mopping up the Celtic warriors on the misty isle of Hibernia. They did name it Hibernia, which very likely derives from the Latin hibernus, which means wintry. It is believed that the Roman General Agricola did consider an invasion and believed that he could conquer the island with one legion. Yet apart from befriending some minor Irish notable in exile, Agricola's intended Roman invasion never got off the ground. There is some evidence of small Roman incursions onto the island, but more of marauding bands from Ireland and Scotland making sorties for plunder into the Roman settlements of mainland

Britain. As a consequence, we had to wait all those centuries until we joined the European Union before we began to contemplate a decent road-building programme.

Recent DNA research has tended to debunk a lot of the old mythology about our racial or ethnic origins, introducing a more credible map of our lineage and diverse make up. There is no doubt about various clan, tribal or religious differences or about the arrival of many groups at different times in our history. The notion of racial purity or tribal uniqueness is pure nonsense. It appears that there is very little in ethnic or racial difference between us and many of our nearest neighbours in Britain, although we have undoubtedly developed very differently from them.

In an interesting new book, 'The Origins of the British', Stephen Oppenheimer addresses the pre-history of Britain and Ireland on the basis of DNA and linguistic analysis. These new tools of modern archaeology throw much new light on the dark mysteries of our past origins and debunk many old theories, strengthening some other mythological notions of ancestry on these islands. Oppenheimer argues that the Celts - or rather the peoples of Ireland, parts of Wales, Cornwall, and western Scotland - rather than originating in middle Europe as previously believed, arrived by sea from Iberia and the French Atlantic coasts many thousands of years before the Iron Age. He does suggest that the deep genetic divisions between some British and the rest of us on these islands arose from their very early genetic links with Scandinavia long before the Viking period. Relatively few would appear to be Anglo-Saxons. His research supports the view that the Celts were a real rather than mythological people, that they existed in many parts of Britain and Ireland long before the Roman invasion and had southern European and Iberian roots.

Another book entitled 'Blood of the Isles' by Bryan Sykes, Professor of Human Genetics at the University of Oxford, makes very interesting reading and draws on DNA as the main source of information to determine the genetic history of Britain and Ireland. His book which he describes as *'the very first book to be written about the genetic history of Britain and Ireland using DNA as its main source of information'* concludes that *'overall, the genetic structure of the Isles (Britain and Ireland) is stubbornly Celtic, if by that we mean descent from a people who were here before the Romans and who spoke a Celtic language.'* He points out that we are an ancient people and are genetically rooted in a Celtic past and concludes from his research that *'The Irish, the Welsh and the Scots know this, but the English sometimes*

think otherwise. But just a little way beneath the surface, the strands of ancestry weave us all together as the children of a common past.'

Now I have to wonder what all the fighting was about for the past eight hundred years in Ireland when we, the 'Celts' might actually have been demanding the return of our full inheritance of the 'Celtic Isles' of Britain and Ireland. What a prospect. I have no doubt the scholars of archaeology and history will in time unravel the great mysteries of ethnicity and race and help us make sense of our cultural roots. But in the meantime, with the hot blood of poor mortals, we must make the most of the real live people that we've got to work with on this small island.

Of course there is no doubt that some of the Fir Bolgs (big-bellied men) are still with us, as are the Dubh Gall (dark foreigners) and the Fionn Gall (fair foreigners). While we missed the Romans, in the centuries that followed these early arrivals we had Danes, Normans, Saxons, Spanish, French, Scottish or Cromwellian and Royalist English settlers all adding to the Irish stew, or what more politely could be described as 'the human tapestry that makes up modern Ireland'.

Norse invader

Dubh Linn- the Black Pool

When Brian Ború led the Munster men to rid the country of the Norse invaders at the battle of Clontarf in 1014, the Danish King Sitric of Dubh Linn watched him with interest. These Danish citizens of the city eventually joined in on the side of the Irish King and threw in their lot with the natives. The new invaders were defeated, but the Danish settlement of Dubh Linn continued to grow and prosper, as did the many other coastal communities established by the Norsemen.

Like most of our cities, Dublin was originally largely a foreign settlement and a forbidden city to the native Irish. That remained the case even after the English took over the city in the twelfth century and continued to pursue a rigid policy of exclusion.

The city authorities proclaimed that 'no Irish man nor men with beards above the mouth to be lodged within the walls of the city'. By parliamentary decree they ensured that 'no Englishman shall have hairs on his upper lip'. The watchers of the city were instructed 'to keep an eye on any Irishman who came to the city' and to 'bring him to the Mayor if he had an immigrant look'. What constituted an immigrant look in those times we can only conjecture, but evidently it was enough to be apprehended.

Yet by the 16th century this foreign enclave had picked up some of the local habits as the settlement was boasting no fewer than 91 public breweries and some 1,180 pubs, approximately one pub to every three families in the city. George Bernard Shaw put this down to the Irish weather, which he maintained *'will stamp an emigrant more deeply and durably in two years, apparently, than the English climate will in two hundred.'*

Galway had some similar experiences, with many restrictions placed on the Catholic or native Irish within the walls of the city. Originally it was the stronghold of the O'Connors, with a castle built at the mouth of the Corrib River by Toirrdealbach Ua Conchobair, The King of Connaught in 1124. In the Anglo-Norman invasion it was captured by the De Burgos, later known as the Burkes, who maintained a major influence over the city for many centuries. The native Irish were excluded from the city and explicitly so by a by-law in 1460.

It developed an impressive international trade and brought great wealth and privileges to traders of the city sometimes referred to as the Tribes of Galway. These included such families as the Lynches, Blakes, Burkes, Martins,

Kirwins and Bodkins etc. who developed commercial interests in the West Indies, in Bordeaux, in Nantes and in Dublin and London. They fell foul of Cromwell when they backed the royalist cause and were displaced by a new protestant establishment who applied rigid penal laws against the Catholic population of the region. Yet today Galway is a thriving trading and culturally strong tourist city with a vibrant young population, an impressive university, NUIG, and other centres of learning and enterprise with no doubt about its Irishness.

More Irish than the Irish

By 1368 the English were so concerned that their colonists in Ireland were 'going native' that they enacted statutes to prevent by force of law the inexorable process of assimilation which had Norman Lords speaking Gaelic, patronising Irish music, wearing native dress, marrying Irish women and becoming indistinguishable from the people they were meant to colonise.

In 1596 Edmund Spencer was to write about the colonists: *'Lord how quickly doth that country alter men's nature.'* He went on to disapprove of the fact that they had become *'even more stubborn and disobedient than the natives'.* Oliver Goldsmith noted that;

'To begin with Ireland, the most western part of the continent, the natives are peculiarly remarkable for the gaiety and levity of their dispositions; the English transplanted there, in time loose their serious melancholy air, and become gay and thoughtless, more fond of pleasure and less addicted to reasoning.'

Cromwell tried to solve the problem by driving the native Irish into the West and populating the South and Midlands with planters from his own armies. His policy of ruthless slaughter of all who dared resist was followed by a policy of banishing the Irish 'to hell or to Connaught', but even that policy did not quite work out as he ordained. A study of blood groups in human genetics by Dr Earl Hackett of Trinity College published some years ago, demonstrated convincingly that many of the Irish-speaking Aran Islanders are likely to be descendants of Cromwellian settlers, who had unequivocally 'gone native'. Certainly, an old friend of mine now deceased, Gaelic poet Caitlín Maude from Rosmuc in the Conamara Gaeltacht, recognised very clearly her Cromwellian ancestory; *'le Cromail a tháinig mo shinsear isteach, thar Sionainn siar…'*

The Statutes of Kilkenny, the Act of Union and the Penal Laws were all attempts to separate the colonists from the native Irish, but they did not prevent the newcomers in many cases from becoming 'more Irish than the Irish themselves'. Indeed it was a completely Protestant Parliament in 1782, known as Grattan's Parliament, which declared itself empowered to enact laws independent of the English Parliament. That independent spirit was to bring about the Act of Union, which abolished the 'Irish' Parliament and reasserted direct English rule from Westminster.

Changing times

The countless references to Ireland as a Catholic country are certainly less than accurate given the number of Protestants of all denominations, Presbyterians, Quakers, Unitarians, Methodists, Huguenots, Jews, Pagans, believers and non-believers alike, who have frequented these shores. Many of them left a significant mark on our society and on our culture and continue to play a central role in modern Irish society. Brendan Behan's shorthand version of Irish people as Catholics or Protestants on horse back was never accurate, no matter how much it felt like that for so many poor Catholics.

In more recent times, we have also seen the growth of the mainly eastern Muslim, Hindu and Buddhist communities with their unique religious observances and distinctive dress. We also have a significant influx of Eastern Europeans and Africans of multi-ethnic origin in recent times. In fact this may not be new, as some evidence suggests that our own predecessors most likely came from the North Africa and Iberian regions many centuries ago, rather than from the supposed eastern European origins of those we once considered our Celtic ancestors.

The Irish Stew – A Most Exotic Mix

'April 17, 1949: Irish republic tonight at midnight. Hilton Edwards piously thanked God that England was free at last from 700 years of Irish domination.'
Micheál Mac Liammóir

The history of Irish republicanism is one of curious evolution. Although the Irish Catholic population has generally embraced a modern Republican form of government, the genesis of Irish Republicanism is deeply rooted in opposition, led originally by Protestants and Dissenters, to British colonial policy in Ireland. From Wolfe Tone to Robert Emmett, Henry Joy McCracken, Jemmy Hope, Thomas Davis, Charles Stuart Parnell, Roger Casement to Douglas Hyde (the first president of the Free State), the list of prominent Protestant figures that espoused the cause of the Irish Republic is certainly impressive. Many actually gave up their lives for their belief in that cause and espoused the radical principles of the French revolution 'Liberty, Equality and Fraternity' in response to the dreadful plight of their Catholic neighbours under colonial royalist rule.

In his sturdy defence of that minority in Seanad Eireann in June 1925 during that historic debate on divorce, the renowned poet, William Butler Yeats, warned the new Free State establishment that,

'if you show that this country, Southern Ireland, is going to be governed by Catholic ideas and Catholic ideas alone, you will never get the North... you will put a wedge into the midst of this nation... I am proud to consider myself a typical man of the minority... we are no petty people. We are one of the great stocks of Europe. We are the people of Burke; we are the people of Grattan; we are the people of Swift, the people of Emmet, the people of Parnell. We have created most of the modern literature of this country. We have created the best of its political intelligence...'

It's true that the Irish cultural and political world owes a lot to that minority who courageously rejected any inherited affinity with the oppressive colonial agenda of the landlord class. Over many generations Irish radical sentiment was often well articulated by Anglo-Irish or Protestant literary figures such as Oscar Wilde and his mother Lady Wilde; by Thomas Davis, Lady Gregory, Seán O'Casey, William Butler Yeats, Douglas Hyde, Jonathan Swift, George Bernard Shaw, John Millington Synge, and many, many more. The same Anglo–Irish component is equally evident in the visual arts, music and all aspects of the culture, politics and intellectual life of this country. The Anglo-Irish certainly have a claim to greater acknowledgment for their part in the cause of Irish independence than many latter-day Irish nationalists care to admit.

The simple equation of Irish and Catholic could never satisfactorily describe the true identity of our people, notwithstanding the statistics. That concept of 'Irish' and 'Catholic' has a more cultural than religious resonance, reinforced in our history by the Penal Laws and the class difference between landless Catholic tenants and their Protestant landlords. During the period of the Land Wars many Catholic tenants were subjected to dispossession and eviction by their Protestant landlords, many of whom did not even live in this country. At a later date some 'strong' Catholic farmers or landlords' agents demonstrated no less ruthlessness in getting rid of unwanted tenants. Ulster proved not to be the Promised Land either for many poor Presbyterians, who were also persecuted for their religious beliefs. As a consequence, hundreds of thousands of them immigrated to North America before and during the Great Famine of the 1840s to escape from poverty and second-class citizenship. Many of them were also Famine victims and shared death and disease in the 'coffin ships' with their Catholic neighbours, in search of a better life in the New World.

The Penal Laws made rebels of the whole Catholic population who were then subjected to inhumane and degrading treatment by the police, bailiffs and land agents backed by the British military and legal establishments. Yet it is ironic that the political leaders of Irish nationalism were very often Protestants and during the Land War, the leader of the Irish Parliamentary Party was a Wicklow Protestant, of landlord stock, Charles Stewart Parnell. Earlier, Protestant leaders of the United Irishmen such as Wolfe Tone and Samuel Neilson fought not only for the interests of their 'own kind' but for Catholic, Protestant, Dissenter or Slave in Ireland or in any other part of the globe. Douglas Hyde, (an Craoibhín Aoibhínn), the first President of the Free State, was a Protestant who worked tirelessly for the Irish language and stated in 1915 that it was his ambition that we would 'use the language as a neutral field upon which all Irishmen could meet.'

In sharp contrast, many prominent leaders of the Catholic Church were less than enthusiastic about the national struggle, the land war or the labour movement. A particularly virulent opponent of 'Fenianism' was Cardinal Paul Cullen who proclaimed in a Pastoral letter,

'As to what is called Fenianism, you are aware that looking on it as a compound of folly and wickedness wearing a mask of patriotism to make dupes of the unwary, and as the work of a few fanatics and knaves, wicked enough to jeopardise others in order to promote their own sordid views, I have repeatedly raised my voice against it since it first became known.'

Iranian restauranteur

He was not alone in his hostility to Irish revolutionaries among the senior Catholic clergy over the years of conflict but it also true that many of the more junior clerics stood resolutely with their people, however rebellious in those troubled times.

Jonathan Swift, the Protestant Dean of St Patrick's and author of 'Gullivers' Travels', could be described as a very reluctant Irishman. He once expressed the view that 'I reckon no man is thoroughly miserable unless he is condemned to live in Ireland'. He is believed to have been born in Dublin in 1667 of Yorkshire descent and belonged to the Protestant ascendancy. Yet, he championed the Irish cause in his own way, supporting human liberty rather than the Nationalist cause, and was a much loved character by the poor and downtrodden, particularly the people of Dublin's Liberties. In an attack on the landlords of his time he wrote:

'It is certainly a bad scheme in any Christian country that there should be beggars at all. But alas! Among us where the whole nation itself is almost reduced to beggary by the disadvantage we lie under, and the hardships we are forced to bear; the laziness, ignorance, thoughtlessness, squandering temper, slavish nature, and uncleanly manner of living in the poor popish natives, together with the cruel oppressions of their landlords, who delight to see the vassals in the dust; I say, that in such a nation, how can we otherwise expect than to be overrun with objects of misery and want?'

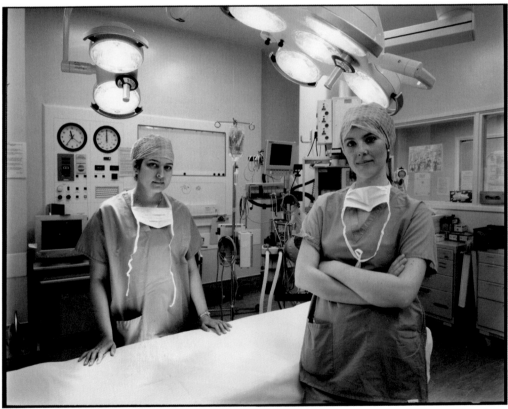

Chilean and Goan doctors

The Irish ascendancy landlord class was a notably obnoxious element in society, described by Arthur Young in 'A Tour of Ireland' as *'lazy, trifling, inattentive, negligent, slobbering, profligate...'* He also pointed out that *'a landlord in Ireland can scarcely invent an order which a servant, labourer or cottar dares refuse to execute. Nothing satisfies him but an unlimited submission.'* A slightly more benign view of that relationship between landlord and tenant was advanced by Sir Jonah Barrington, *'At the great house, all disputes among the tenants are then settled – quarrels reconciled – old debts arbitrated; a kind Irish landlord reigned despotic in the ardent affections of the tenantry, their pride and pleasure being to obey and support him.'*

Undoubtedly, it was that despotic landlord culture, the religious persecution, the heavy-handed suppression of dissent and the sectarian misrule, which nurtured Irish radicalism and republican sentiment. The poor Catholics were in town and country, the most oppressed though not exclusively so, but it was the intellectuals of the ascendancy who gave a political voice to their dissent and shaped the essential character of militant Irish Republicanism from the days of the French Revolution in 1789 to the establishment of the Republic.

The Society of Friends

'The Quaker community is of interest for comparison with other minority groups having a certain amount of cohesion, with the Jewish community for example or the Huguenots, even with the aristocracy, each of which developed their own tradition and behavioural code. The amount of material still to be sifted and assessed in relation to the Quakers in Ireland is immense and the references in State papers, news papers and literature generally have scarcely been touched'
Maurice J Wigham, author of The Irish Quakers

Filipinos on parade

Growing up in the Liberties in Cornmarket, our nearest church was the Church of Ireland St Audeon's, one of the oldest churches in the city, it stood cheek-to-jowl with its Catholic neighbour on High Street. The Catholic Church – now the headquarters of the Polish Catholic community in Dublin – dominates the skyline, but shares virtually the same territory between the Forty Steps and

Schoolhouse Lane. The dark shadows of the two medieval churches were a constant reminder to us as children in the Liberties of the historic enmity of the two major religious congregations in Ireland. The predominance of that historically fractious relationship served to obscure from us the many more complex relationships between the differing positions and traditions of the Protestant, Dissenter, Jewish or non-believer groups all around us.

One small group of migrants, who came to our shores and in my view have made a disproportionate contribution to our society over many centuries and indeed continue to do so to the present day, is the Society of Friends, better known as Quakers. In my area of the Liberties of Dublin, they established an early and honourable presence in the community by providing much needed services for the local people. It was in the Liberties that the Quakers founded the first crèche in Ireland. The sign is still proudly on display in Meath Street.

They are also known for giving men and women equal place in their Society, consistently opposing war and actively supporting peace on this island and abroad. I remember attending peace meetings in the Eustace Street Meeting House, now the home of the Irish Film Centre, where Dr Noel Browne and a number of other 'dangerous radicals' were given a hearing when many other venues were closed to them. I have always found Quakers supportive of the peace movement and less addicted to the rhetoric of war than other Christian denominations. In the 1960s and 1970s many Irish Quakers were involved in organisations such as the Irish Voice on Vietnam and the Irish Pacifist Movement, a small branch of a worldwide organisation called Resistors International. Brenda (Meredith) Yasin, the mother of my partner Rosheen, was secretary of the IPM for many of these years.

Originally associated with Puritanism and the Cromwellian plantation of this country, the Irish Quakers gradually emerged as a distinct religious group with their own ethics and benevolent disposition. They also suffered their own persecution for their beliefs from both the established churches and civil authorities of their time, with many of their number jailed in Ireland and Britain. One such Quaker was Edward Burroughs who died in Newgate Prison in London. He wrote:

'Oh, Ireland, I bear thee in mind, In my soul to thee much love do I find
In thee have I laboured, not sparing my own life
The good in thee to gather which God had made full ripe'

Quakers, through a simplicity and integrity in religious and business practice – the latter being based in the concepts of fair prices with prudent investment and industry – became very successful merchants, manufacturers and bankers in Ireland. Joseph Pyke of Cork, took over a small shop from his father who was previously a farmer. He traded in wool and linen and became involved in shipping. He became very prosperous, gaining a reputation for fair business practices, yet he curtailed these activities in favour of family and religious commitments. He wrote:

'I do not ever remember that I ever broke my word or promise with anybody, neither did I venture more in one ship than I was able to bear if it was lost, for I did not then, nor do I now, look upon it as just to venture or hazard other men's substance, let the profits be ever so great.'

Portuguese pose

They did not confine their transport activities to shipping, from sail to steam, but were also early investors in the railways. Thomas Pim was chairman of the first Irish railway company, which established the Dublin and Kingstown (Dún Laoghaire) line in 1834.

In Clonmel, Jacob and Grubb built stationary steam engines for milling, but it was Richard Pim who built the first Irish locomotive, called Princess. Many other Quaker families became involved in the railways such as Samuel Haughton who was also a director of the Dublin Kingstown line. Those early Irish locomotives became known as the Quaker engines, surviving for many years on our rail system.

It was during the Great Famine of the 1840's that the Quakers played a critical and invaluable role in Irish society in famine relief and in active representation in the US and Britain on behalf of the victims. Joseph Bewley, who died after months of gruelling work trying to help famine victims, worked closely with Jonathan Pim and hundreds of other Quakers in a variety of genuine relief efforts.

In a paper on those events published in Studies in 1950, Thomas P. O'Neill points out that:

'The real merit of the activities of the Quakers, at least their greatest ultimate value, lay not in the immediate steps taken to alleviate distress but in the approach to the fundamental economic causes of poverty in Ireland. The number whose lives they saved will never be known, but their views on land tenure helped to mould public opinion'.

Had they never distributed relief, the publication of their reports would have justified the eternal gratitude of the Irish people. It should be no surprise therefore that Rowan Gillespie of Quaker stock is the sculptor of the impressive Famine sculptures outside Dublin's Custom House, and their sequential arrival pieces on the other side of the Atlantic in Toronto, Canada, on the shore of Lake Ontario. It's also worth remembering that that city, then with a population of only 20,000, accepted 38,000 famine refugees from Ireland. Some 1,100 of the 'wretched' Irish died on the lakeshore. So did many natives who sought to give help and succour to the new arrivals. Does today's Ireland have a serious migration problem by those standards?

Rowan's first cousin is Rosheen Callender, the National Equality Secretary of SIPTU, who is my partner. Their grandfather, James Creed Meredith, who became a Quaker on marriage, was President of the Sinn Féin courts during the War of Independence. He later became a Supreme Court judge and Ireland's representative at the Saar plebiscite in 1934. He also contributed to the drafting of the Irish Constitution, Bunreacht na hEireann, of 1937.

Many prominent Quakers helped to shape the nature of modern Ireland and in spite of their small numbers continue to make a significant contribution to Irish life and business. Names such as Bewley, Allen, Webb, Wigham, Shackelton, Haughton, Pim, Myers, Meredith, Marsh, Jacob, Cadbury, Lamb, Rowntree, Newenham, Pierce and Leckey, Bulmer and Hobson, have a resonance in this little country over many generations. In my childhood we believed that the Santa Claus in Pim's store in Georges Street was the only authentic Father Christmas, and all the others only pale imitations. Not only Kerryman Tom Crean, but also the exploits of Len Shackelton of Quaker stock, were a great source of pride when I took an interest in the famous explorers of the world and in particular their expeditions to the Antarctic.

Shaping life

An interesting anomaly in the Society was Katharine Norton, born MacLaughlin, an able minister in Barbados. She was a Gaelic speaker who preached in Ireland on a number of occasions in the 1680s, introducing the concepts of Quakerism to the native Irish speaking population although the practice of proselytising was not generally associated with the Society of Friends.

The Jewish Community in Ireland

'The rights of Jewish citizens as equals among the other denominational groups are expressly recognised in a special clause of the Irish Constitution-probably the only Jewish community in the world to be constitutionally protected in this explicit manner. In practice, too, the Jews of Ireland have always felt free from discrimination. In fact, Ireland is one of the few countries that has never blemished its record by any serious anti-Jewish outrages'
Chief Rabbi Immmanuel Jakobovits, 1949

Bloomsday has become one of our great days for literary celebration in the capital city, marked every June 16th in memory of James Joyce's classic novel, Ulysses. The central character is a somewhat unlikely Dublin Jewish gentleman, son of a Hungarian Jewish father and an Irish Protestant mother. Some of the narrative in the novel relates to differing attitudes to nationality and race which has engaged Joycean scholars and historians alike and has often raised issues in relation to the Jewish community in Ireland, in particular the question of anti-Semitism.

In one episode, Bloom, talking with John Wyse, expresses the view of persecution that *'all the history of the world is full of it. Perpetuating national hatred among nations.'* Asked what was his nation, Bloom is unequivocal. *'Ireland, says Bloom. I was born here. Ireland.'* He is equally adamant that he also belongs to a race that *'is hated and persecuted, this very moment, this very instant.'*

In a letter to The Bell, an important literary journal of the time edited by Seán O'Faoláin, Gerald Y. Goldberg, subsequently Lord Mayor of Cork, insists that Joyce was no anti-Semite, and also that *'there have been Jews in Ireland for hundreds of years and that the present substantial communities of Dublin and Cork have been in existence for upward of a hundred years without fear of molestation and in amity with their fellow Irishmen.'*

That relatively small community has the distinction of producing Lord Mayors for the three cities of Dublin, Cork and Belfast, all positions requiring democratic election to the councils by the citizens of those cities. The history of the Jewish community in Ireland, sadly somewhat depleted now, has been well documented by Bernard Shillman, Louis Hymman, Dermot Keogh and more recently in Cormac Ó Gráda's 'Jewish Ireland in the Age of Joyce'.

My friend and union colleague Manus Ó Riordan, who comes from that neighbourhood off Dublin's South Circular Road known to us as little Jerusalem, has also written extensively on the Irish relationship with that once thriving community. Active persecution does not appear to have been the general experience of Jewish people in Ireland, although the issue of anti-Semitism did arise from time to time when issues of trade, commerce or financial dealings caused a reaction from other vested interest groups. Undoubtedly, there were problems arising from the practice of money lending in poor districts, but there were Jews on both sides of the argument just as there were Christians. Dublin 'diddly' clubs were well named because of their uncertain pedigree as saving institutions generally organised by Irish Catholics. The banks have little to be proud of when it comes to usurious charges, nor have the many other moneylenders prior to the arrival of the credit unions.

Bloomsday

In 1904 there was a serious attack on the Jewish community in Limerick inspired by a Redemptionist priest, Father John Creagh, and unfortunately supported by Arthur Griffith, the founder of Sinn Féin. In 1899 Griffith wrote in the United Irishman that the three great evil influences of the century were the *'Pirate, the Freemason, and the Jew'*. Griffith appears to have concentrated his energies on the Irish Nationalist cause, but frequently was less than generous about the rights of others.

But the most serious anti-Jewish activity, which in my view should not have been tolerated by any self-respecting Irish Government, was the behaviour of Charles Bewley, a vigorous anti-Semite, who was the Irish envoy to Germany under the Nazis in the 1930s. Appointed Irish consul to Berlin in 1921, he demonstrated his prejudices at a very early stage of his diplomatic mission. In his memoirs Robert Briscoe, an active participant in the war of Independence who later became Lord Mayor of Dublin and the first Jew elected to Dáil Eireann, complained about Bewley's behaviour at a Jewish café in Berlin, from which he was forcibly ejected.

Signs of the times

His later activities as Consul during the Nazi era are much more serious, and are well documented by Dermot Keogh in his book 'Jews in Twentieth Century Ireland'. Bewley, from the famous Quaker family who converted to Catholicism, did little to assist Jews who wished to seek refuge in Ireland and in his reports to the Irish Government sought to play down the threat facing the Jewish population in Nazi Germany. As a consequence, the role of the De Valera government is highly questionable in relation to Jewish refugees and asylum seekers before, during and after the Second World War. As a country that puts such emphasis on human rights and religious freedom, we can take little pride in our responses to that terrible period for the Jewish people on mainland Europe.

Much earlier, many Jewish people had come to Ireland following pogroms in Russia in the 1880s and 1890s. Others came from Poland, Germany, Holland, England and Lithuania. Initially many shared a common cause with the Catholic Irish in their desire to achieve emancipation. From the time of his election to the House of Commons, Daniel O'Connell supported Jewish emancipation and worked closely with Issac Goldsmith, leader of the Jewish campaigners in Britain, in the campaign to recognise freedom of conscience. In 1828 he supported Goldsmith in attempts to establish legal rights in Britain for his community and stated; *'Ireland is the only Christian country that I know of unsullied by any act of persecution against the Jews'.*

The Jewish people of Ireland made a very significant contribution to our national development, both economic and social, and were part of our communities. My father was on very friendly terms with Bob Briscoe. Sam's shop on Francis Street was well known to us as children, as were the many Jewish 'rags, bottles and jam jar' merchants. For our labours, in an early form of rubbish recycling, they often furnished us with the money required for 'the fourpenny rush' in the Tivoli Cinema.

A more serious contribution to the fledgling industrial economy of the state was made by Fred Hitchman, a Jewish emigrant from Vienna who, in 1933, founded the tannery in Carrick-on Suir, which was named Plunder and Pollock at the request of the Irish government. The tannery was a huge success, employing over three hundred workers in its heyday, rising to over one thousand from mergers and expansions, until business mistakes and the consequences of incompetent management brought about its demise in 1985, long after the untimely death of Fred Hitchman in 1965.

His family owned a considerable tannery in Leitmoritz just inside the Czech border, from which Fred came to Ireland in his early twenties with his uncle Richard and his mother Irma to develop the Carrick-on-Suir enterprise. Later he was able to assist other family members to flee from the Nazi occupation and brutality. He was a very unusual employer in that he actually encouraged the organisation of trade unions in the tannery and on one occasion actually picketed the Dáil with his employees over a threatened failure to deliver coal to the tannery that would have resulted in considerable hardship for the workers.

Harry Kernoff, the renowned Dublin artist, described himself as 'partly Russian, partly Spanish, partly Jewish but mostly Irish'. I got to know Kernoff when he sold copies of his famous woodcuts of the city and its characters in the Dublin pubs for very little money, and had the privilege of visiting his studio in Stamer Street with my brother Séamus, who was a good friend of Kernoff's.

We had a family connection with Kernoff because he made an impressive woodcut of my uncle Jack, a one-time leader of the Dublin unemployed. The woodcut was used by Leslie Daiken, another Jewish Dubliner, to illustrate a book of poetry and ballads that he edited called 'Good Bye Twilight', published in 1936. Kernoff also painted my brother Tom in the helmet of the Dublin Fire Brigade. Tom served in the brigade for many years and subsequently wrote its history, 'The Dublin Fire Brigade'. Harry Kernoff, who depicted my city with so much character and genuine feeling, continues to remain for me, one of the most evocative and insightful of all the Dublin artists.

The Italian Connection

'The Irish, after all, are only Italians who don't mind the rain.'
Vincent Caprani

Another small but interesting group, well established in Irish society North and South, is the Italian/Irish community, who managed to integrate very well into Irish life over many centuries while preserving their own distinct customs, and in many cases their own language. Yet many of that stock are authentic Dubliners with little to distinguish them from their neighbours other than their undeniably Italian names.

The Italian/Irish community found a niche in opening most of Dublin's early fish and chip shops. Good solid food at a reasonable price, I always considered Burdock's, my own genuine Liberties version owned by an Irish family, to be the 'real' Dublin chipper, but Burdock's was definitely an exception. The majority of chippers, providing the genuine poor people's choice of cuisine, were run by Italians, as were the early ice-cream parlours.

The Italians have a special claim on that specifically Dublin expression, the 'wan-an-wan'. It evolved as a result of the mutual difficulties the 'Dubs' and the 'Eyeties' had in making themselves understood to each other, and the famous phrase developed denoting one portion of fish and one portion of chips – a 'wan-an-wan'.

On the other end of the culinary scale, Italians and other immigrants opened some of Dublin's most famous up-market restaurants, including the first of the so-called ethnic restaurants, such as the Golden Orient in Leeson Street and The Delhi (subsequently The New Delhi) in Camden Street. Along Merrion Row and Baggot Street, you had the two extremes: at one end, the exclusive Unicorn, which had been opened in the early 1940s by a Jewish couple who were refugees from the war-time pogroms in their native Austria, and at the other end, the Polish-Scottish owned café run by Margaret Gaj that was the refuge of every left-wing student and impoverished radical of the 1960s.

The Italians have a long and interesting pedigree on this island since Christopher Columbus dropped in on his journey in search of the new world. Apart from the many ecclesiastic visitors from the Vatican, who featured prominently in our history for better or worse, Italian workers came here in search of a better life over the centuries. The Italians brought art, the music of the opera, great literature and the classics to our shores and have continued to do so over many generations.

Moto Italia

The skill of Italian craftsmen is evident in many buildings from the 18th century onwards. Castletown House in Kildare was designed by one Alessandro Galilei, and the great Georgian decorations in the big houses, particularly the ornate plasterwork, owe a lot to the Francini brothers, Paul, Philip and Bossi. Giovanni Battista Cipriani designed the south-end window of Trinity College in 1771.

Another Italian, known for his contribution to developing the transport sector, was of course Charles Bianconi, who introduced what's been known ever since as the 'Irish back-to-back cart', which provided a form of public transport throughout the length and breath of Ireland. In the second half of the 19th century, these carts were used mainly to run people between the towns and the railway stations – well before the arrival of CIE. Bianconi was also a close friend and supporter of Daniel O'Connell in the struggle for Catholic emancipation.

Joe Nannetti was the first Labour Lord Mayor of Dublin and was associated with another Italian named Menotti Caprani, who worked for the Freeman's Journal.

Art curator

They were well known to James Joyce and feature in Ulysses, in the scene where Leopold Bloom enters the case room of the Freeman's Journal: *'He pushed in the glass swing door and entered, stepping over strewn packing paper. Through a lane of clanking drums he made his way towards Nannetti's reading closet'.* Spotting Mennotti Caprani he makes the observation *'Caprani too, printer, more Irish than the Irish'.*

The inheritance of Joyce, Nannetti and Caprani are well represented by my friend and trade union colleague Vinnie Caprani, writer, raconteur and Dublin wit, author of 'A Walk Around Dublin', and 'Vulgar Verse and Variations, Rowdy Rhymes and Rec-im-itations'. Vinnie incorporates the Italian-Irish connection into a distinctly Dublin persona: *'I draw my pride from the Liffey side because I am a Dub.'* Vinnie goes on to lay further claim to his full national inheritance as a true blue Irishman in his rhyme The Dubliner:

'I boast of noble lineage – I know it off by heart!
Sir Tristan and Isolde, and King Conor Mac Art
For I'm Gael and Norse and Norman stock, and Huguenot moreover;
I'm Sitric blonde and Strongbow brave, and Scion of Danish rover.
I'm Palatine (came from the Rhine) I'm Flemming and Walloon;
I'm soldier, sailor, jarvey, tailor; I'm pikeman and dragoon,
I'm a weaver from the Liberties, a sawyer from Portobell-a,
I'm a butcher boy from Ormond Quay, I'm a rag-and-bones 'oul fella'
I'm the olive skinned Eye-talian man that invented 'wan-and-wan'
Or the Hebrew hawkin' haberdash from dawn to setting sun....'

Orange and Green

*'Great Empires have been overturned. The whole map of Europe has been changed…
The modes of thought of men, the whole outlook on affairs, the grouping of parties all
have encountered violent and tremendous changes in the deluge of the world. But as the
deluge subsides and the waters fall short, we see the dreary steeples of Fermanagh and
Tyrone emerging once again. The integrity of their quarrel is one of the few institutions
that has been unaltered in the cataclysm which has swept the world.'*
Sir Winston Churchill in the House of Commons 1922

Ulster pride

Since the creation of the two states of Ireland in 1921 the 'Irish Question' has
revolved around the issue of the Protestant majority in Northern Ireland claiming
British citizenship and the minority Catholic or Nationalist community generally
asserting their Irish identity and allegiance.

This difference is an integral part of our long and tragic history, and is still very
real for people in Northern Ireland. It is overlaid with sectarianism, bitter memories,
and misconceptions, which make the two communities prisoners of their own
past. Although they share a common history and a common Ulster identity, their
loyalties are very different, which has often made them more antagonistic to each
other than they are to any external group in Britain or Ireland.

Orange versus Green has become the popular depiction of the Northern Ireland conflicts, with the Orange Order or Orangeism being a central component in the defence of the Protestant tradition in Ireland. Originally, this group was involved in agrarian confrontations with groups such as the Roman Catholic Defenders in the 1790s. There were earlier Boyne Societies, formed in commemoration of the victory of William of Orange over the Catholic King James at the Battle of the Boyne in 1690. It is worth remembering now that the Pope of the time also celebrated that victory, with little if any concern for the consequences that battle might have for the Catholic members of his congregation in Ireland.

Officially the Orange Order came into existence in 1795 and since then has played an active role in many sectarian confrontations with Catholic communities, particularly but not exclusively in Ulster. As a consequence of these confrontations and their seemingly insatiable need for marching in a never-ending militaristic display of their 'loyalist' Protestant credentials, most Catholics resent their antics and their sectarian activities.

Their frequent marches and their 'Kick the Pope Bands' are viewed as a deliberate provocation of the Catholic nationalist community, particularly during the 'marching season' of July and August. In the minds of Catholics, the Orange Order is synonymous with Protestant triumphalism. Their sectarian behaviour serves as a constant reminder of the British conquest, the colonization and the dispossession of the native Irish from their lands and the denial of their nationhood. I often wonder if this ritual celebration could ever become an occasion for a common expression of civil and religious liberty or a happy occasion for all citizens to share the entertainment and join in the festivities?

On parade

It must also be acknowledged that religious sectarianism has never been confined to the Protestant majority in Northern Ireland. Catholic political leaders have also cynically used it as a true and trusted device to maintain their own political and religious hegemony in a ghettoised and seriously divided society. Religion has, for centuries, been ruthlessly employed as a political weapon in Northern Ireland by both communities and as a consequence, we now have a very divided society there. In our turbulent history, sectarianism has been a convenient first resort of political scoundrels, switched on and off at will to perpetuate their power and often to facilitate a cynical denial of peoples rights.

Chinese traders

Historically, Ulster was the strongly Gaelic part of Ireland, the land of the O'Neills and the O'Donnells. It became the home of English and Scottish settlers who eventually outnumbered the indigenous population after the departure of O'Neill and O'Donnell in 1607. More than two million acres of fertile land in Ulster were occupied by Protestant English and Scottish settlers, often very industrious farmers with a strong loyalty to their Protestant faith and their country of origin. They were put there to guarantee the political union with Britain and to keep the natives in check. As a consequence, assimilation with the native Catholic population never came about, and thus the seeds for later conflicts were sown deeply in the Ulster soil.

Recent political developments have raised hopes for a historic compromise between these settlers and their disposed neighbours, with the full endorsement of the British and Irish governments and the support of the leaders of both traditions in Northern Ireland. Great strides are being made by the power sharing administration but a more enduring local trust and inter communal co-operation may be slower to develop. There is great hope that that will eventually happen but nothing about Northern Ireland can be taken for granted. I have no doubt that such a coming together in Northern Ireland would also have very positive consequence for all those on the island who favour a new beginning based on equality, respect and pluralism.

When the new Northern Ireland Assembly elections took place in 2007 one interesting result emerged in Belfast that must encourage all who are genuinely committed to integration and diversity. That was the emergence of Ms Anna Lo, a Hong Kong born social worker, as a successful candidate for the Assembly. Although elected for the middle class and university district of Belfast her constituency also includes the more working class areas of Lower Ormeau and Donegal Roads, areas of some relatively recent racist activity.

Mrs Lo's success was doubly heartening because it signalled not only the prospect of a new tolerance for people from a totally different background, but also the emergence of a political representative for the Chinese community, an important group dispersed throughout the island. It also brought back to me personal memories of the Chinese Restaurant on Ship Quay Street in Derry City, where many protagonists adjourned for respite, Green and Orange, after civil rights marches, until some 'super patriot' destroyed this small but important oasis of inter communal sanity.

While the Chinese have a reputation for remaining within their own close knit community they have integrated well in Irish society and play an important and growing role in our economy. Their numbers are increasing, notable from the numbers of new Chinese Restaurants, but also from the growth in student numbers, technicians, medical personnel and general trade and commercial dealings with China. A friend from Bray told me a few years ago that the town has attracted so many Chinese that the joking name is now 'Brayjing', and it has on occasions been said that Mandarin Chinese might well be the second most widely spoken language in Ireland.

Polish Footballers

Perhaps Polish might have a stronger case these days. As I write, an estimated 200,000 Polish are now in Ireland and the number is growing. Many are working in the construction industry, but they have established themselves in shops and other enterprises throughout the country. The weekly newspaper, the Polska Gazeta, is not yet sold in mainstream newsagents, but has a circulation of some 7,000 nevertheless. The newspaper serves as a forum for discussion and offers information and support for the Polish community, including free consultations with union representatives, solicitors and financial experts.

Travellers, the Real Outsiders!

'The marginalisation of Travellers in Irish society is acknowledged by people of varying political positions and approaches. Past policies, while designed to overcome this marginalisation, have sometimes exacerbated the situation because of a failure to grasp the nature of the oppression experienced by Travellers'
John O'Connell, in Racism and Anti-Racism in Ireland

The group that is perhaps the least integrated in Irish society is unquestionably and wholly of Irish descent, of the Catholic religion, bearing familiar names, familiar to us all and very much part of our tradition in both town and country. Yet the Travellers are very much a group apart. They have their own customs and dialect, known as the Gammon or the Cant, and a series of clans with complex family relationships and at times dangerous antagonisms that can descend into feuding and violence.

Some believe Travellers are descended from those driven off their land by Cromwell, but there were nomadic people in Ireland well before Cromwell. In the past they were predominantly horse dealers and tinsmiths, fortunetellers, casual farm workers, traders and scrap dealers. Some of them were musicians, entertainers or trick-of-the-loop characters that you meet at fairs or festivals. Now more of them are poor people who live in deplorable conditions on the side of Ireland's roads. There has never been adequate provision of facilities to cater for this relatively small nomadic group, nor has the community at large shown a willingness to accommodate their different life style.

The 'better off' now travel in highly decorated caravans and tend to be antique dealers or traders. Some of them have become very successful business people, but many others are still dependant on welfare or handouts. Travellers continue to have a very low life expectancy, poor health and related problems because of their life style and lack of adequate services. The 2002 census also revealed that an astonishing 73% of male travellers and 62% of females were unemployed. This compared with an average rate of 8-9% across the whole population.

As with all categories of people, Travellers are individuals with different characteristics, yet most settled people tend to stereotype them as a nuisance, dirty, untrustworthy and certainly unwelcome neighbours. Our local authorities generally have a poor or at least sluggish record of providing adequate services by way of halting sites and the basic necessities of civilised living, and only reluctantly acknowledge their nomadic way of life. Publicans rarely want to serve them and many hotels find reasons to refuse their custom despite the equality legislation, which specifically prohibits discrimination against members of the travelling community.

In recent times the involvement of some Travellers in serious criminal activities, drug dealing and violence, has not helped to ameliorate the existing antagonisms. But the settled community has more than its fair share of criminals, a fact that doesn't reflect on it in the same racist way as it does on Travellers.

While a lot of good work is being done by their own organisations, such as Pavee Point and the Irish Traveller Movement, a major comprehension gap continues to exist between Travellers and the settled community. Over many years voluntary, religious and statutory authorities have sought to address the problems of travellers such as accommodation, health, education and welfare, with only limited success.

On the road

In my view, there has not been sufficient emphasis on their economic role, and the need to facilitate their legitimate development of alternative employment opportunities consistent with their nomadic life style. I have always wondered why we did not encourage them more in their traditional role of recyclers and waste metal recovery dealers as well as in their craftwork and unique cultural heritage.

In the sphere of traditional music I know of the incalculable contribution of such musicians as Ted Fury and his son Finbar, uillean piper and singer, and all of their family. Likewise the Keenans, and the many others before them such as Johnnie Cash, Johnnie and Felix Doran, or Johnnie Collins the singer and storyteller.

I have great personal memories of evenings spent with Joe Donoghue in Cherry Orchard who welcomed all and sundry into his tent during the demonstrations against evictions on that site. I have a great regard for the courage and tenacity of other Traveller activists I've met, such as Rosaleen Mc Donagh and Michael Collins and their colleagues in the Travellers' movements.

This small minority of distinctly Irish people is reputed to amount to less than 30,000 in Ireland, although there are also several thousand others scattered across Britain and farther, in the United States, mainland Europe or even Australia. They are a legitimate segment of Irish society. Some of their organisations argue convincingly that they are an ethnic minority, and should be treated as such.

Whatever of their origins and their past, they deserve far better treatment and respect than they currently experience. In turn, members of the travelling community must themselves find new ways to develop a better relationship with the 'settled' population and seek opportunities to increase the awareness and understanding of their aspirations within the wider Irish society.

I have always believed that equality of treatment should not depend on goodwill or kindness. You may not exactly 'love your neighbour' but you must find a tolerable way to live with him or her. Equal rights and equal opportunities should be acknowledged as fundamental to the way we live, something to be shared with all who choose to be involved with us. Otherwise we ourselves become damaged or diminished by the unequal relationships we tolerate. Given the short time we all get to live in this world, we might keep in mind that we are all travellers of sorts, essentially passing through.

The New Nation – Cherishing all its Children

So who are the 'real true blue Irish'? Are we seriously in danger of being overwhelmed by the latest arrivals on our shores? Are we some pure racial group in danger of extinction like a plant species incapable of adaptation to facilitate survival in changing circumstances? Or are we Catholics, Protestants, Methodists, Presbyterians, Dissenters, Jews or Gentiles, (or now Poles, Latvians, Nigerians, Brazilians, etc.), and can we now accept the common name of Irish, as Wolfe Tone hoped when he sought *'to abolish the memory of all past dissentions and to substitute the common name of Irishman in place of the denominations'*.

Remember the Doyles were once the Dubh Gall (dark foreigners), from Scandanavia, and the Finns the fair ones. The McDowells and Dougals were Scottish Gallowglasses. The Fitzpatricks, Fitzgeralds, Fitzwilliams, Fitzsimons and Fitzmaurices, Burkes, Barretts and Butlers were all Norman invaders. The Barrys were Welsh; the Allens were Scots or French. The multi-coloured names of Browns, Blacks, Whites, Grays, etc. were immigrants, as were the Walshes, the Scotts and the English. The Lynches are Normans and the Lyons and Moores are very likely English. The O'Flahertys and the O'Malleys were pirates.

In fact if you go back far enough, from the Celts onwards, we are all a little bit foreign, blow-ins from the four winds. Given the suspect nature of all our roots, I'm personally attracted to the simple yet profound response of Joyce's Leopold Bloom to the question 'what is a nation?'

'A nation?' says Bloom. *'A nation is the same people living in the same place.'*

We the Irish are certainly the same people, but not always in the same place. We are a combination of all the diverse elements that went to make us what we are. St Patrick was very likely Welsh, Patrick Pearse's father was an Englishman, Jim Larkin was from Liverpool, James Connolly from Scotland, Countess Markievicz was born in London and married a Polish count. Erskine Childers (whose son became President) was English, yet he brought the guns into Howth for the Easter Rising. Seán Mac Bride, one time republican leader and later international statesman, was born in France.

Nuala Ní Dhomhnaill, our leading Irish language poet, was born in Lancashire. Míchael Mac Liammóir, the dramatist and actor, was actually Alfred Willmore from England. Paul Henry, one of our most loved landscape painters, was an Englishman. It's hardly possible to construct a completely insular 'national identity' with so many 'external' accidents of birth.

Taoiseach Bertie Ahern, when speaking in Westminister to the joint houses of parliament on the 16th May 2007, pointed out that *today there are over one hundred members of this Parliament with an Irish background. And there are millions more like them in Britain, who have gone on to new levels of success with each new generation. And of course the tide was not all one way. There are over 100,000 British citizens in Ireland now, a most welcome part of an ever more diverse population.'*

An file

Eamon DeValera is a particularly interesting example of the 'More Irish'. Saved from execution by the British in 1916 because of his American citizenship, his family origins have remained mysterious. Born in New York he arrived in Ireland with his Irish-born mother and the historians claimed his father was a wealthy Spanish businessman. But one academic at Colombia University, Brendan Ward, claims to have tracked down his true family origins to Mantanza, a rural province in Cuba. He also claims to have met members of the De Valera family who look distinctly like De Valera, and to have traced Baptismal, Communion and Confirmation certificates of his father to this area.

Whether the origins are Cuban or Spanish it is interesting that none donned the mantle of Gaelic Ireland more completely than Eamon De Valera, the man who could look into his own heart to see what the Irish people wanted.

'Blow-ins' have been the very substance of Irishness, from Cork to Donegal. Another colourful fellow was His Highness the Maharaja Jam Sahib of Nawanagar, better known as Ranji Prince of Cricketeers, who bought up Ballinahinch Castle in Connemara in 1924. Ranji was mad keen on fishing, as well as cricket, and he applied his great wealth to keeping palaces and properties in India and England, as well as landscaping the gardens and woods of Ballinahinch and erecting fishing piers and huts along that part of the river in Connemara.

Ranji became known as the Maharaja of Connemara and was an extremely popular man locally. He would arrive home to Ballinahinch every summer, around June, bringing five motorcars (two limos and three smaller cars) and, when returning to India in October, would give the cars away as gifts to the locals. He did this every year until his death in 1932. If anyone has wondered about the unusually high motorcar density in Connemara in the 1930s, there's your explanation.

Ranji also held an annual drinks party on his birthday for all his staff, both Irish and Indian. He served his guests himself and by all accounts they all got on very well together – not just when intoxicated but throughout the year! At the end of the birthday party, he had transport at the door to bring everyone home – so he was ahead of his time on the drink-driving issue too.

Another exotic Easterner who came to our 'showers' was the man reputed to have introduced the word 'shampoo' into the English language. His name was Sheik Deen Mahommad. Born in India in 1759, he was a former member of the British Bengali army who served with a young Irish officer named Godfrey Evan Baker. When Baker returned to Cork, Mahommad came with him and married an Irish girl named Jane Daly. He studied the English language and literature, and wrote one of the earliest travel books about India, still considered a remarkable achievement for that period of 1800. He used the name Dean Mahomet in Europe and is considered to have been the first Indian entrepreneur and professional to settle in the west. He had an obvious acumen for business as he secured many financial subscribers for his book and drew on his own knowledge of Ayurvedic medicine to establish himself as a masseur and private doctor.

The 'shampoo' connection arises from his use of the Hindi word 'champa', to press, associated with head massage. He eventually called himself the 'shampooing surgeon'. In 1807 he and Jane moved to London where they opened the Hindustani Coffee House, not an entirely successful venture as it eventually led to bankruptcy. Undaunted, he headed for the booming resort town of Brighton where he set up an exotic bath house offering special treatments, shampoos and massage and vapour baths. He was an Indian Muslim who brought knowledge and skill from East to West, overcoming racial prejudice of the time in defiance of the Rudyard

Kipling axiom of colonial supremacy, *'East is East and West is West and never the twain shall meet.'*

Cork has another interesting link with the Orient, particularly for those with a sweet tooth. That is the delicious Turkish Delight produced by the Hadji Bey company in Cork. Apparently in 1902 a Mr Batmazian came to Cork to exhibit his produce at the Cork Exhibition on the Carraigrohane Road. He was a Christian Armenian who had escaped to London to escape from Turkish persecution. Although he had studied law in Constantinople he had poor English and little money.

To survive, he took to producing and selling Turkish Delight under the name Hadji Bey. This particular confectionery has been known since the 15th century and is made from a mix of honey, grape molasses and flour. Finding a good response to his product, he decided to stay and set up his business. The name of Hadji Bey has been synonymous with Turkish Delight ever since, and has been produced in Cork by a succession of enterprises. The latest was established in 2004, capitalising on the worldwide reputation of this unusual Cork cross-cultural delicacy. The name comes from the name of Haci Bekir, who was the first confectioner to use sugar and cornflour to improve the texture of the product and was subsequently appointed as chief confectioner to the Ottoman Court. A painting of Haci Bekir in his shop by the Maltese artist Preziosi hangs in the Louvre in Paris.

Another interesting family of somewhat uncertain origin but who had a huge influence on our society is the Guinness dynasty. Clearly identified as part of the Anglo-Irish ascendancy, with lords and ladies and an umbilical cord to the British monarchy, they played no small part in determining who we are today. It has been suggested that they were descendants of a Cromwellian officer called Ghennis but the family prefer the claim that they were descendants of The Magennis clan from County Down who fought with King James at the Battle of the Boyne.

Whatever their origins, the beverage they produced and still produce has a long association with our people. Since 1759 they have been brewing the black stuff at James Gate, in the heart of Dublin, and selling pints of it in great numbers to the plain people of Ireland at home and abroad. In turn, almost as a patriotic duty, they have promoted the product everywhere they went, made it famous in song and story and extolled its virtues to all in sundry. It's not surprising that it travelled the world with the Harp, one of Ireland's great symbols, (also used now by Ryanair) and managed to convince the populous that in all circumstances it truly 'is good for you'.

Mongolian chefs

Apart from Aer Lingus with their successful use of the Shamrock, that other great Irish symbol, I can think of no other product which over the centuries could became synonymous with a people to the extent that Guinness did. Yet, the company remained generally a loyal British institution, supported the British monarchy, recruited for and from the British army and contributed in no small way to the expansion of the British imperial influence in many distant lands. Yet, it must be said in their favour that the Lords and Lady Iveaghs certainly left an impressive legacy in employment standards, health and housing, welfare, parks, mansions, charitable trusts and culture in Ireland and Britain. It has been said that over generations, food and no doubt drink, is often a more enduring symbol of nationality than language or culture. If that is the case, Guinness, long before the advent of Diageo, the multi-national drinks company, made an enduring mark on the Irish people. As Miles na gCopaleen pointed out all those years ago *'A pint of plain is yer' only man.'*

Nowadays, of course, we have tremendous diversity and a choice of exotic food and drinks in our many ethnic restaurants. Where would we be without our Chinese or Indian takeaways, our Japanese sushi bars, Turkish kebabs, American Burger joints, the Italian home-delivered pizzas and the wines of the universe? Now we are spoiled with our choice of quality foods from all corners of the globe. International access to the wonders of world music, sport, entertainment, arts, literature and culture are also guaranteed by our access to television, radio and the Internet. A return to splendid isolationism is no longer possible or desirable. However, we have much yet to do if our society is to facilitate a truly egalitarian order that genuinely accepts diversity and equality for those who bring that great wealth of exotic choice.

On our doorstep we now have Afro-Celtic bands, Indian Pipers, Japanese fiddlers, Irish-speaking Nigerians and Chinese in the Gael Scoileanna, and many overseas specialists, scientists, technicians, doctors, nurses, artists and writers working in our midst. The process of change and integration is constant and more visible than ever before. Equally, the reverse is true with the Irish expansion into all the attractive holiday or business destinations in Europe and beyond. We have become the property entrepreneurs of the European Union and beyond with our insatiable hunger for bricks, mortar and property ownership. We have little cause for any nostalgic dose of retrospective xenophobia given the benefits we have derived from our foray into the global economy and our obvious ability to benefit now from the investment opportunities in every other economy in the world open to us.

Many of the people helping to build the New Ireland can claim a multiplicity of origins, beliefs or nationality. Some may choose to remain and become citizens, but many more may not. The former president of the Irish Medical Organisation, Dr Asim Ishtiaq, is Pakistani; Michael Flatley of Riverdance is American. Dr Kadar Asmal, the leader of the Irish Anti-Apartite association and later a government minister in South Africa, is a South African Indian, Moosajee Bhamjee, also a South African Indian, was Labour TD for Clare, a traditional Fianna Fail stronghold, for a number of years. His colour and his racial origins proved not to be an electoral disadvantage. Although considered not to have a chance prior to the election, he was the first of the candidates elected to the 27th Dáil in 1992. Bhamjee was educated at the College of Surgeons in Dublin and married a local girl from Cooraclare. While there were many jokes about his election, the most astute in my opinion is that *it was good to see an Indian among the cowboys in the Dáil.*

The town of Portlaoise in county Laois elected the country's first black Mayor in June 2007. It reminded me of the election of a voluntary or charitable mayoralty in Blackrock, in County Dublin some years ago, which was won overwhelmingly by my good friend Logan Raju, a Malaysian Indian restauranteur. Councillor Rotimi Adebari of Portlaoise came to Ireland from Nigeria in 2000 as an asylum seeker and was elected to the local Council, although not yet an Irish citizen. When accepting the chain of office he is quoted as saying that *'I say this to my fellow immigrants: the sky is the limit. Ireland is not just the country of a thousand welcomes but a country of equal opportunity.'* He added that *'embracing diversity'* would be the theme of his term of office. I can only wish him well with that mission.

Dr Said Ahmed Yasin, Rosheen Callender's father, was the Honorary Consul General for Pakistan in Ireland. Born in the Punjab in 1917, he came to Ireland to study Veterinary and Agricultural Science in 1937. He returned to India in 1945, before the 1947 Partition of the country, which saw the creation of Pakistan as a separate state from the newly independent India. Having married Brenda Meredith

Teachta Dála

from Dublin, he spent some time with the Pakistani civil service and the United Nations Food and Agriculture Organisation but returned to Dublin in the mid-1960s as a lecturer in Trinity College's Veterinary School.

Said, who lived for many years in West Cork, often told the story of an Indian Sikh who came to Ireland at the same time as himself from the Punjab. He eventually gave up wearing the Sikh turban, but not before he took the precaution of getting a series of photographs of himself wearing his traditional turban. These were used in subsequent years to reassure the family at home, with regular pictures, that he had not deserted the traditional faith.

Pakistani cousins

That issue of the Sikh turban has emerged as serious issue with wider significance more recently, with the decision of the Garda authorities not to alter their uniform dress code to facilitate the wearing of the Sikh turban. I sympathise with the general argument that the Gardaí, as an important part of civil society should avoid being identified with particular religious denominations. Yet, that has not always been the case and we can hardly claim that we have maintained an exemplary consistency in the separation of church and state in this country. Rather we have traditionally opted for accepting religious symbolism in all walks of life and a wide public manifestation of the catholic ethos in many civic institutions.

However, I do believe that the greater good will be served by attracting more members from the newer communities into the police force. It's very important for both the Irish authorities and the migrant communities to actively try to resolve these issues of cultural and religious identity, in the context of a mutual respect for each other's traditions and a more positive approach to integration and acceptance.

My favourite 'odd job' tailor is a black Dubliner from Cabra, Jude Hughes. He has a lot of insightful experiences of racism and colour consciousness in the city, but he takes the optimistic view there has been a general improvement in attitudes as people become more familiar with new migrants of all different shades and denominations.

Before the recent wave of migrants we had a number of mini-colonies throughout the country. I well remember the initial wonderment and fascination with which the Japanese employees of Asahi were received in North Mayo and the towns of Ballina and Killala. Another unlikely group of Mayo men were those Pakistanis associated with the meat baron Sher Raffik of Halal Meats, who built his own small mosque in Ballyhaunis and became a major force in Ireland's meat processing Industry. Arklow Pottery became part of the Japanese Noritaki and attracted numerous Japanese workers to the County Wicklow town, to the great curiosity of the local workers. We had an influx of Dutch and German people in the '60s and '70s into West Cork, and Killarney too has its share of Germans, associated with the crane factory. Monaghan has its Latvian mushroom pickers and many towns and villages have become accustomed to strangers associated with local factories in foreign ownership.

Japanese artist

These are the more obvious examples because their appearance and language often marks them out. Less obvious though more numerous are the returned second or third generation Irish emigrant families, the British and American English speakers who are now a very significant component of our management and general labour force in today's Ireland. In every parish we have returned emigrants or their children often only identified by their very different accents or outlook on life.

There are many, many more new Irish of all shapes and sizes, a normal spread of humanity no better or no worse than the homogeneous varieties. The census of 2006 shows a growth of 8.1 per cent in four years in the republic's population with a steady migration in recent years of 46,000 in excess of our emigration each year. They come to work and earn their keep. Some will gain public notoriety for reasons good and bad but most will naturally integrate over time into Irish society.

We have always lived with a great variety of accents, with different politics and loyalties and personalities of very different origins. Yet in their own diverse and

American expertise

unique ways, many of those who first came here as strangers have contributed to the reshaping of modern Ireland and brought many valuable attributes to their adopted homeland. We are all the richer for this revitalising influx, which is evident in virtually every sphere of national endeavour from the economy to culture, sport, and cuisine and even trade unions or employer organisations. Indeed, it could be argued that to choose your country and to make a personal investment of oneself in that society is a more deliberate and compelling option for nationality than any mere accident of birth.

Race - the Power of Illusion

A novel, interesting and unusual approach to the question of race was adopted by a Californian Newsreel production in three parts entitled RACE-The Power of Illusion. This video production scrutinises where the idea of race came from and how it took hold of our minds. In a hard-hitting and extremely informative analysis it sets out ten things that everyone should know about race.

Firstly it points out that race is a relatively modern concept and that the English language did not have a word for race before 1508. In ancient societies people were distinguished by physical distinction, religion, status, gender, class or language but not by any supposed racial difference. It argues that there is no characteristic, trait or even gene that distinguishes all members of one so-called race from all the members of another so-called race. While elsewhere in this narrative I point out that DNA has been used to trace the movement of peoples, that research does not support the existence of separate races or nationalities based on particular human characteristics. Despite appearances there are no separate subspecies or races. Skin colour is only skin deep and the genes determining skin colour have nothing to do with hair, height, athletic ability, or forms of intelligence etc. Most genetic and other differences exist within 'racial groups' rather than between them. Slavery and conquest predates race and had nothing to do with any belief in natural inferiority. Curiously enough the concepts of race and freedom evolved together.

'All men are created equal... endowed by their creator with certain unalienable rights...' The American Constitution, 4th July 1776

Yet that constitution was drawn up for a society that had an economy based on slavery and needed a racial justification to sustain it. Over the years racial difference has been used to rationalise inequality, conquest and exclusion or even extermination of 'other people' black, red or white. Race is not biological but it can still determine the distribution of opportunities and resources. Colour blindness will not end racism but to combat racism we need to identify the social and economic policies, the deep rooted institutional practices and the ignorance and stereotyping that sustains the advantages of one group over another because of some perceived yet illusionary difference between people.

A report to the European Parliament in 1995 pointed out that;

'The history of racism in Europe includes many different examples of ideas based on particular scientific and political theories, religious convictions and other cultural manifestations (the arts). The corrective action of democracy through non-governmental organisations is therefore extremely important in combating racism and xenophobia within society. There are clear limits to the role of Government...'

It went on to argue correctly in my view that we have to create *'conditions where all members of society realize that ethnic and cultural diversity of contemporary Europe is ultimately a source of measurable benefit...'* setting out the EU's task as one of encouraging *'people to live together in a variegated and diverse society, in a way which promotes, rather than destroys mutual respect.'*

Europe of the Nations

Our membership of the European Union has had a profound impact on the national psyche and liberated us from the tyranny of introspective defensiveness based on an unhealthy preoccupation with the legacy of British misrule in Ireland. Europe made all the difference to us because it created a new place and a new space for us to expand and grow in our own right. In spite of our initial apprehensions we took, as ducks to water, to the wider European economics, politics, social policy and increasingly, environmental concerns. Apart from military or defence issues, more often not related to NATO, we have played a full part in the European project, at times gaining benefit from Britain's euro-scepticism which has at times made them very reluctant Europeans.

At the heart of the European project is the issue of nation states sharing sovereignty, accepting different languages, cultures and history. It was born out of two disastrous world wars, which resulted in the death of tens of millions of people, combatants and non-combatants alike. That nightmare still haunts the people of Europe and has determined much of its politics in a way that we often fail to fully appreciate because of our relative isolation from those conflicts. We did suffer the loss of many thousands of Irish combatants, but have only recently begun to accept their sacrifices as a legitimate cause for commemoration and respect, if not full endorsement.

In more recent times there has been a growing concern at the revival of racism, ultra nationalism and xenophobia in many countries, with the particular experience of ethnic cleansing, racist slaughter and genocide in the former Yugoslavia. Race riots in Paris and the whole concept of a 'War on Terror', the consequences of the Iraq war or 9/11, added to the continuous repression and fighting between Israel and the Palestinian people, have brought the threat of religious or racist conflict nearer home.

The right to protest

There is a general increase in racial violence in many European cities. The first report published by the EU Agency for Fundamental Rights pointed to a notable upward trend in racist crime in Germany and France. While the report noted that only four states of the current twenty-seven actually collect comprehensive data; France, Germany, Austria and Sweden, there was a reported increase in racist attacks in eleven member states between 2001-2006. In France and Germany the racial attacks are clearly associated with extreme right wing groups and neo-Nazis. The report 'Racism and Xenophobia in Member States of the EU: 2007', calls for more systematic recording of data and concrete measures by member states to counteract this trend.

Given this worrying development and the knowledge that few countries have actually eliminated the causes of racist or religious bigotry, we face a serious challenge to develop a real harmony within our diverse communities that would enhance the European experiment of 'unity with diversity'. Ireland can succeed with its own integration process, but we require a very conscious process of nation building, based now on the emerging needs of our more diverse population.

The EU has set down many guidelines in reports, legislation, directives and regulations, including inter-state agreements and protocols, but recognises that Governments require the support of the ordinary citizen to counteract racism. Yet there is still considerable ignorance about racism and a lot of fear and insecurity about racial differences, which needs to be explored in more public discourse here and throughout the EU.

Irish Racism

'For over forty years I have carried within me, like a dull ache, both the reality and the imminent possibility of being found unacceptable on the basis of culture and on the basis of the colour of my skin. This has shaped and marked me. My perspective on racism in Ireland is personal, rooted in my own experience and in the knowledge I have gained from living in Ireland for more than twenty years…'
Gretchen Fitzgerald, in Repulsing Racism, 1992

It's often very comfortable for us to consider racism as a foreign phenomenon, something that has little to do with us unless others turn it on us. Yet, all the elements of prejudice, insecurity, fear and ignorance, which feed racist attitudes, are present in our society.

More importantly, it's within all of us, however liberal we believe we are. It is part of that inner self that we need to constantly interrogate and redefine as the world around us changes. We are all more comfortable with the familiar family values we grow up with, the memories, experiences, symbols, places and people. As we grow older this frame of reference expands to incorporate new experiences, new perceptions and new people. For most of us that inner development has a very strong element of exclusiveness based on our inherited value systems and limited exposure to other people, mores or cultures.

As we grew up we all picked up prejudicial views about Red Indians, Black Jungle 'Savages', Japanese, Arabs, not to mention Brits, Prods, Tinkers or Homosexuals.

The list is endless and can include people from down the street, around the corner, from another school or county. Most of these views change with time, but they can also be reinforced by bad experiences or deliberately cultivated prejudices, many encouraged by planned campaigns of propaganda.

Ukrainian architect

Power relationships are generally at the heart of racist attitudes. Racism becomes a dangerous and potent force when these sub-conscious attitudes are exploited to support someone's 'power agenda'. Exploitation is often at the heart of the matter because if we accept some groups as less equal than others you can justify inferior treatment. Race, creed, colour and gender have all been used in turn to justify inequality and unfairness in society. They can also be whipped up to generate irrational fears.

Leaders of warring states often seek to justify unjustifiable wars of attrition by an appeal to some morally superior notion of civilisation to explain the slaughter.

The enemy 'without' often provides a convenient justification for the abuse of power within. Hollywood has usually obliged with suitable film material to support military or police violence, at home or abroad. Equally, religion and ethnicity has often been used as a readymade weapon for tyrants of different colours and creeds. We have all seen the spectacle of religious notables of many persuasions, proclaiming the noble gospel of 'peace and love' while blessing the weapons of war for their own military establishments.

I'm old enough to remember the supposed threat of the Chinese Yellow Peril, the Domino theory of South East Asia, the squinty-eyed Japanese, the Reds who will murder us in our beds, the Wild African Tribes, the Red Indian Savages looking for white men's scalps. It was never admitted that it was actually white men who robbed the land and resources of these people and in the process initiated many of the most barbaric practices of extermination and blood letting. Headhunters, cannibals and barbarian tribes of all nationalities were depicted as a constant threat to our Christian or White Anglo-Saxon (and therefore superior) civilisation, engendering deep fear and racial prejudice in most of us.

More recently the 'War on Terror' of George Bush and Tony Blair, no matter how unintentional, served to restore the centuries-old fault line between Christianity and Islam in the Middle East. That doctrine, supported by military might, has effectively turned many Middle Eastern countries into war zones, rekindling old enmities and creating increased religious zealotry and mass murder. All of this mayhem in other people's countries is presented as a defence of democracy or 'our way of life'. They could do well to remember the words of President John F Kennedy when he said *'The basic problems facing the world to-day are not susceptible to a military solution.'* Kennedy also endorsed a very different kind of war, in 1963 when speaking at the World Food Congress he said, *'The war against hunger is truly mankind's war of liberation.'*

Another seriously objectionable concept from the recently created Washington neo-con think-tank at the White House is the 'Old Europe' versus 'New Europe' label as a litmus test for friendship with America. The dangerous, military backed globalisation process of these ideologues, based on US unilateral expansionist doctrines, developed by back room supporters of President George Bush, has serious implications for all of humanity. They are not supported by the majority of Americans, who have very little influence on their country's foreign policy, yet it is paid for with the lifeblood of young Americans. Neither are they supported by most member states in the UN. Yet unfortunately, the bigoted 'fundamentalism' of some right wing Christian groups in the US associated with these doctrines, has

Palestinian soldarity

97

not been lost on many disadvantaged people in the Islamic world and has greatly assisted the spread of their own militant brand of 'fundamentalism'.

They have assisted the rise of 'fundamentalists' of all creeds who have such vested interests in antagonism and conflict. I have personally found the most difficult discussions on racial or religious prejudice are those associated with the Israeli Government and the Jewish people in the Middle East. Criticism of Israeli policies by anyone, however genuine their support for human rights, brings a reminder of

More Irish

the Holocaust and those making any critical remarks about Israel are accused of anti-Semitism. This makes it difficult to challenge Zionist policies however provocative or repressive they may be. I believe that racism is not exclusively a weapon of anti-Semites and should be exposed wherever it occurs. No historic experience should be accepted as a justification for its use in today's world. Otherwise, we are laying the foundations for future wars of mass destruction and extermination of many more innocent people.

Because of our history as a subject nation we Irish often assume that we are not particularly racist or intolerant of other religious and cultural groups. We even have a grand traditional ballad to make the point for us, The Galway Races, sung with such great gusto by the late Luke Kelly...

'There was half a million people there of all denominations,
The Catholic, the protestant, the Jews and Presbyterian
There was yet no animosity, no matter what persuasion
But Fáilte and hospitality including fresh acquaintance'

That spirit is today evident at the Dún Laoghaire Festival of World Cultures and long may it last. But, whatever our propensity for welcoming geniality on such festive occasions, we cannot pretend that we are immune from racial prejudice. We have been lucky in recent times, though certainly not in the past, that we are not particularly threatened now by racial hostility from elsewhere, or have reason to fear racial prejudice from our neighbours.

However, neither have we reason for complacency. All of that could change if we were now faced with a serious downturn in our economy. Racism or racial prejudice is no longer a remote notion of the external world, but a serious domestic issue requiring constant attention and understanding. Some of our recent responses have been less than exemplary in that regard, so let's hope the new challenges can, in the future be met in a more enlightened manner by Irish people and particularly the powers that be.

Stephen's Green

A man walked past me in Stephen's Green,
Amazing how like me he was:
Just the same height, the same build,
Wearing, like me, a grey-green gabardine,
Wearing, like me, glasses,
Bearing, like me, books,
His lower lip, like mine, large-
And there's the difference:
I reckon his might be firm,
Not loose like mine.
For he's what is called black,
And I'm -take a look in the mirror-
What is often called white.
How long can he like this burg
Where the glic might call you
'pathological'
for challenging words like
'nigger'?

Or should we wear yellow this winter?

Pearce Hutchinson
By kind permission of the author and The Gallery Press, Loughcrew,
Oldcastle, County Meath, Ireland, from Collected Poems (2002)

Working on the railway

How are we coping?

Picture the scene, Saturday night in a bar in rural Ireland, everyone having the craic and availing of the late bar. In this bar were some local farmers discussing things that farmers discuss. It was late, one farmer was getting ready to go home and he said to another, 'It's time to go, I have to milk in the morning.' 'Milk, on a Sunday morning? You're mad,' replied his friend. 'I have a young Ukrainian slave to do that for me. You should get yourself one. It's the best thing that ever happened in Ireland.'
Anton Mc Cabe, Navan, Siptu Anti-Racism Group, describing a case he dealt with in 2005

Though there are also good reasons to have confidence in the basic decency of most people, some of the cases I have heard of would make me ashamed to be Irish. Among hundred of cases reported to me, the one which struck me with

particular disgust concerned the Filipino housemaid employed by a well-to-do Irish family who worked long and hard to prepare the Christmas dinner, and was then asked to leave the house on Christmas Day as they had visitors for dinner. Apparently there was 'no room at the Inn' for that Christian woman.

Siobhán O'Donoghue of the Migrant Rights Centre Ireland (MRCI), referring to a report on migrant women employed in private domestic employment in Ireland at SIPTU's 2005 National Women's Forum on 'Organising Diversity', pointed out that the research demonstrated in stark terms that *these women are frequently underpaid, working excessive hours, expected to carry out degrading tasks, have little or no access to medical and social supports, are subjected to severe levels of social control and are vulnerable to becoming undocumented'*.

For these reasons I was particularly pleased to see that the Government has accepted a statutory Code of Practice For Protecting Persons Employed In Other Peoples Homes, prepared by the Labour Relations Commission, in accordance with the commitment negotiated by the trade unions in the social partnership agreement Towards 2016. The Code was the result of several years' campaigning and lobbying by Siptu, the Irish Congress of Trade Unions and the MRCI. It sets out the minimum conditions which are acceptable in Ireland in respect of the dignity of their work, living arrangements, privacy, social life and their entitlement to have clear terms of employment such as pay rates, hours, duties, annual leave, place or places of work, etc., but however welcome it is, it is not enough.

While these provisions represent a good exposition of entitlements for domestic workers there is a distinct need for a statutory means for enforcement and a very active inspectorate to police it. Would we need all this paraphernalia if we treated people working in the home as we would like to be treated ourselves?

Overall, though, there have been some significant turning points in our experience of migration. The influx of asylum-seekers in the late 1990s did cause alarm in some quarters, in Ireland as elsewhere; were we taking more than our share of the world's refugees, would the social welfare system and our economy collapse, and – as always –would they take our jobs?

There were certainly outbursts of racism. But there were also many examples of genuine gestures of welcome in local communities, such as the weekly session in a Cork refugee centre started by local musicians, on the grounds that music was a universal language that required no translator. The incident that touched many hearts with pride in our generosity was the campaign in 2005 of the students at Palmerstown Community College to reverse the deportation of Kunle Elukanlo to Nigeria. With placards and deputations, and the backing of Archbishop Diarmuid Martin of Dublin, the Palmerstown students argued that Kunle was not only a fellow student, but a friend, and should be allowed to return to sit the Leaving Certificate at least. Not many win a battle with the

Afghan hunger strikers

Department of Justice, but the Palmerstown students succeeded, and Kunle was allowed to return and took the exam successfully.

The occupation of St Patrick's Cathedral in May 2006 by Afghan asylum-seekers also focused our attention on the realities of the refugees' lives. Frustrated with the perceived delay in dealing with their applications for asylum, 41 Afghans converged on Dublin from Cork, Kerry, Mayo, Limerick and Kerry.

Nine of them were minors and were removed at an early stage. The remaining men went on hunger strike, and over the next fortnight the protest brought out the worst but also the best in us. There were ugly demonstrations outside the cathedral with placards demanding 'send them home', and groups of up to 30 people chanting 'let them die'. There were bitter verbal attacks on foreigners who were 'stealing our jobs'; despite the fact that one of the protestors' grievances was that they were not allowed to work.

The widespread media coverage, however, raised our awareness not only of the desperation and fear of asylum-seekers, who declared they would commit suicide rather than face deportation, but also of their dreary conditions in isolated centres, jobless and friendless in a strange country, coping with a confusing legal system.

The protest could have ended in tragedy but was resolved peacefully because it was handled with care and compassion by both the Church of Ireland and the Gardaí and all of us became a little wiser in the process. I hope that we have learned that we face major integration issues, which cannot be resolved by reacting to recurring crises in the usual style of Irish pragmatism without reference to a clear and sustainable long-term policy in all our institutions. Irish public policy is still somewhat ambiguous about integration and appears to be uncertain of how to respond to the complexities of the new circumstances.

The 2006 annual report of the Migrant Rights Centre places the problem in the proper context and sets out the nature of the challenge facing us:

'...none of the affluent nations can manage their economies without immigrants. Their contributions range from doing the service jobs that the local population do not want to do, to doing work that the local population are not trained to do. Yet all those affluent societies, Ireland

included, do not seem to value the contribution immigrants make to their economies. Many of the affluent nations complain about irregular migration but are unwilling to develop appropriate migration policies that are dignified and risk-free for immigrants. This indifference to the worth and value of immigrants is borne out by the fact that no affluent nation has signed and ratified the UN Convention on the Rights of all Migrant Workers and their Families.'

The report goes on to tell us that the core of every immigrants experience is uncertainty, tension and exclusion in society, summed up in the experience of; *'Birth in one place, growing old in another place, and feeling a stranger in the two places.'*

Putting a spin on things

It's the Economy Stupid!

The recent population changes in Ireland are of course strongly linked to our economic performance and will, in the long term, be shaped by the evolution of that economy. It's about jobs and work and who will do them. Migration has been generally good for our economy, but not always so good for the migrant.

Various estimates have been made about the numbers of recent immigrants arriving on our shores, most of which are likely to be somewhat inaccurate. FÁS point out that non-nationals constitute approximately 11 per cent of the current labour force, and the Department of Social and Family Affairs figures show that more than 330,000 PPS numbers have been issued to workers from the new EU member states since enlargement. CSO statistics suggest that labour force figures underestimate the overall numbers because of the massive increase in student numbers from EU and other states, such as China and India, and do not include the many family members who do not register for work.

According to FÁS, foreign nationals account for 30 per cent of the total number employed in the hotel and catering sector, 13.5 per cent of the construction sector and 13.4 per cent of the manufacturing sector. That constitutes a major contribution to our economic activity and one that has contributed in no small measure to our overall economic success. These are the new 'breakfast-roll workers' so visible in all our towns and cities or on the farms and factory floors.

The National Skills Strategy estimates that we will need another 310,000 migrants by 2020, assuming a labour force of 2.4 million, made up of 640,000 from our own education system but an additional 310,000 coming from abroad. Whether or not those estimates prove accurate, we will inevitably continue to see a significant influx of non-Irish nationals for short or long-term stay in the years ahead. Undoubtedly a major recession would make a difference to the numbers but would be unlikely to reverse the overall trend in migration.

This poses challenges in relation to language skills in Ireland. A study by Barrett and McCarthy in 2006 found that immigrants from English-speaking countries tend to earn the same as Irish workers, while those from non-English speaking countries were estimated to earn one third less. The language question is also a major issue of concern in our schools as migrant children enter our under-resourced national school system. Some reports have indicated that in schools with either a very small or very large quota of foreign-born children, language skills develop more slowly than in those with a more balanced mix of native and foreign-born.

Equally, language is an issue for those providing social or financial services for an increasingly multi-lingual society. FÁS pointed out in their Labour Market Review in 2004 that knowledge of English 'could be the most important factor in helping someone to get a suitable job'. State institutions and public and private sector employers alike will have to respond to the need for far more language training combined with access to good translation services. Who will provide all these new services is another question that requires serious consideration, but it appears to me that there will have to be a good mix of public, private and voluntary provision. All of us have a role to play in this regard.

Cheese makers

On a more positive note, the new pool of workers with other languages does provide a valuable resource for exporters or importers requiring language skills for businesses in trade or commerce, marketing, sales and services. This combined with the educational achievements, skills and training background of the immigrants provides Ireland with an important 'people' advantage for future development.

My personal problem, I'm sure shared with others, is that I'm finding it increasingly difficult to find make myself understood in pubs and restaurants with my Dublin accent, clearly a diminishing asset in the cultural life of our capital city. But this is our opportunity to learn patience and the art of distinct enunciation.

The work permit system for migrants from outside the EU has not been satisfactory for many workers and has led to significant abuses by unscrupulous employers. The renewal of those permits is also a serious issue as many such permit holders become undocumented, often inadvertently. Because of the growing skills shortages a new Green Card system has been introduced by FÁS to attract highly skilled workers from outside the EU. This is targeted at people expected to earn over €60,000. That initiative recognises the scarcity of high skill in many areas and is a necessary addition in the drive to up-skill the existing labour force to produce a steady supply of high quality workers in an even more competitive era. It remains to be seen how successful this initiative will be but it is an improvement on the old work permit system of virtual 'bonded labour', which gave the employers all the options.

There is a strong argument for the benefits we would all gain from a much fairer international order and less social disruption associated with large-scale worker migration. Most people would prefer to avoid forced economic migration and could do so if we developed more effective economic strategies that placed greater emphasis on balanced and sustainable development in the areas of greatest need. Fairer trade conditions would help, as would investment in areas of high population density or underdevelopment.

Freedom of movement also needs to be balanced with proper labour

Currach race

A German view

market regulation and domestic measures to counteract the ruthless exploitation of migrants. Where good standards are applied to all workers and active steps are taken to prevent exclusion or marginalisation for the indigenous population, the integration of new arrivals is made much easier. We have a lot to learn from those European states that have experienced anti-migrant racism and allowed the emergence of migrant ghettos with high levels of poverty, unemployment and social deprivation.

I hope many of our new arrivals will have the opportunity and the resources necessary to return home some day, to a better life, bringing with them a very positive view of Ireland and the Irish people they met during their sojourn here.

The European structural funds do assist the process of raising living standards within the EU and trade agreements with third countries also play an important part. But the issues extend far beyond the boundaries of the European Union. Hopefully also, the renewed emphasis on sustainable economics and global warming could help us to create, of necessity, a more people friendly and eco-friendly form of economic development. I do find it somewhat ironic that some of the more vigorous advocates of the classical market based globalisation are also the most nationalistic and hostile on migration or environmental regulation.

While we strengthen the instruments of the European Union, which facilitate easier movement for work or leisure or education, we must not allow free movement of capital and labour to create a 'race to the bottom' in employment standards. The recent debate on the EU Services Directive raised many of these issues because of the Commission's attempt to undermine existing employment standards by allowing service providers to apply the standards of the country of origin, rather than accept the standards in country where the services are delivered.

That means changing the emphasis from the 'super-market' concept of Europe to one of a co-operative community of European peoples joined together in a stable political union. While the single market is an important component of that union, it must function within a rational people-friendly social and political environment.

Investment, public or private, can also be used to assist the process of more regionally balanced development by creating jobs where people live, rather than requiring the migration of millions of poor destitute people. When problems arise from that mass relocation of labour it is always the poor migrants who are blamed rather than those whose financial interests effectively create the crises.

Our national efforts at serious regional rebalancing have been particularly feeble to date, with opportunistic decentralisation of public servants rather than genuine local devolved democracy or development policies. The problems of Shannon Airport are a symptom of the short term economic thinking which facilitates development in certain areas of population in the east of the country while other regions loose their population. Ireland needs joined-up government just as we need joined-up thinking about all of these issues. In the wider European context, as at home, we do need to maintain strong regional and social incentives to counteract the tendency towards concentration in over centralised urban areas. But most of all we need to promote the value of people living together in a diverse society, where ever the live, in ways that promote rather than destroy dignity and mutual respect.

Waves of Humanity

'There are no overall certitudes in Ireland any more. There's a lot of diversity of thinking, a lot of uncertainty a lot of trying to assimilate to other cultures. It's a time when we need to take stock, to look into our hearts and find a sense of Irishness, to find a pride in ourselves that will make us sure of what we are.'
Mary Robinson, Uachtarán na hÉireann, 1990

Just as the waves of the sea continually rush to our shores, waves of humanity have washed over this little island for many centuries. Some have come as conquerors, others as exploiters or proselytisers; but more are carried on the tide of necessity seeking a better life in our country. What could be more familiar to us, the Irish, who are the world's migrants, than people coming in search of a better life?

Our Green Isle has many different shades of green and an impressive array of other colours as well. We're a sturdy race of people formed by a fusion of many different ingredients and a proven ability to absorb new arrivals. We were always more varied and more diverse than we tend to acknowledge. Much of our newly found confidence owes its origins to the ability to turn diversity to our advantage.

Would we be a better country without having produced Paul McGrath, Phil Lynott or Samantha Mumba? Would our communities be better served without Chinese Restaurants, Italian fish and chip shops, and Indian or Asian fusion restaurants? How would our hospitals manage without Indian and Pakistani doctors, Filipino

Whiskey in the jar

nurses, Spanish and Latino catering staffs? People of all creeds and denominations are shaping this island community yet we have only recently begun to recognise, with somewhat belated generosity, the true breath and diversity of our society.

We would certainly be less efficient, less interesting and less dynamic as a society if we had preserved an isolationist mentality. Racist attitudes usually arise from fear or ignorance and are fuelled by stereotypes or perceived threats. Our greatest fears about foreigners usually prove to be groundless or at least no greater than the homegrown variety. Also, the more we strive to understand the background and the needs of the new arrivals, the more we can learn about ourselves.

We can in this way sometimes begin to recognise the real needs of the previously excluded people already in our midst. In getting to know the new arrivals as individuals we can also begin to appreciate their individuality and accept them as real human beings in the truest sense. We might eventually be able to expurgate some of our more irrational fears of mysterious strangers; we might in time even enjoy their company, their laughter and their music.

Making music in Kenmare

Ethnically Cleansing the Orchestra.

We'll have no foreign instruments
Away with the cymbals
A bang and a clash,
We're cleaning out the orchestra,
Let's throw out the trumpet
Along with the trash.

We do not want these instruments
Get rid of the shakers
The xylophone too,
They're not of Irish origin,
The horn and the oboe
To name but a few.

They are not welcome anymore
The timpani, tuba,
The flute and cello.
Return home to your countries.
The trombone, the bassoon
And all things mellow.

We do not want no Spanish guitar
No loud African drums.
The end is quite near.

Eh, sorry, are we clear?
Oh–there's no music here?

Vivienne Sullivan. Loreto College, Clonmel
(This poem received a merit award from Poetry Ireland
in the 2006 schools anti-racism competition).

The New Irish

'Here we are thrown back upon our smallness-
From this spot Brendan sailed into the majesty of sea, the mystery of self.
Here on the edge of our old ways we stand bewildered-
Voices urge us to catch the wind, test and tempt us to take off into the old, the new.'
From 'Pilgrim Spirit', by Brenda Yasin

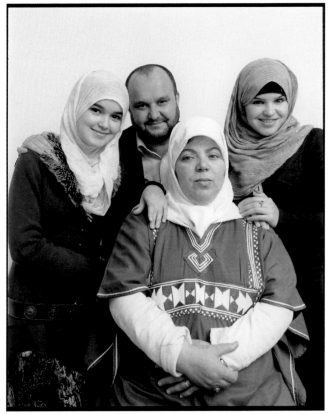

Algerian family doctors

Our new Irish community is very different from the one most of us have grown up with. There are more of us now than there has been at any time since 1861. Our population has increased at a rate of 8 per cent in four years, 2 per cent per annum. Most of this generation rightly expect to be able to live and work in their own country or to travel if that is their choice. They are accustomed generally to meeting people of different colour and creed at work or everywhere they socialise, including an estimated 32,000 Muslims from forty different countries, a new challenge for an overwhelmingly 'Christian' society.

Irish young scientist from Somalia

Many of our new Irish may have different dietary requirements, dress codes, and attitudes to modesty, cleanliness and physical contact. As they come from different countries and regions, there may also be animosity or hostility between groups and attitudes towards class or creed that are not to our liking. We cannot treat them like a new version of the all-purpose 'Protestants', the convenient term covering a multitude of difference. 'Foreigners' won't do either, as more and more native-born Irish are Black, Muslim, Hindu, Buddhist…what better argument for Wolfe Tone's dream of us accepting the common name of 'Irishman or Irishwoman'.

Already many of our institutions and organisations have absorbed thousands of these 'New Irish', or perhaps 'New Europeans' is a more correct description. Now we face the challenge of providing for them in a more structured way, recognising their needs and their individual differences. We cannot avoid addressing any inadequacies in our domestic provision of services and promoting a positive integration rather than swelling our ghettos of deprivation, where new arrivals are expected to compete for the bottom of the social exclusion pile. Although many of the newcomers may only be short-term visitors, many others are likely to remain with us for a long, long time.

At Home in Ireland

"Home is where the heart is", an old Irish proverb

We are a motley bunch, wherever we came from. Now we are, for better or worse, thrown together and have to make the most of our new circumstances on this damp and misty isle. When considering what would best describe the kind of Ireland that I would wish live in, to bequeath my children and to all our future generations, I came to the conclusion that 'An Irish Home' is that place. A home is what we must be for all these in need of love, shelter and a sense of belonging. We of this generation are charged with making and maintaining that home, as a safe place, a place of human warmth and acceptance, a place of sharing, of encouragement and support, a place where everyone can be different but never fear rejection.

We must create that sense of homeliness for everyone in the country without distinction and adopt the values we want in our own home to inform our dealings with others. It is those values, already well understood, which should form the foundations of our civil society, our approach to others and our system of governance. If everyone feels included, and acknowledged as part of that society, the problems of welcoming others becomes less daunting. I could not think of a stronger or more worthwhile identity for modern Ireland than 'The Home of The Irish', or all who wish to be Irish.

Given the millions wanting to be part of what we are, with a real historic claim to that privilege, or the New Irish who are willing to work and share with us now and in the future, we owe it to ourselves and to all of them, to create that home-place now. We have to achieve integrated communities built on co-operation and good neighbourliness. We have the resources and the people to do it, what we need henceforth is the will and determination to make it happen.

I believe we have little to fear and everything to gain from welcoming these optimistic newcomers, working with them and acknowledging the value of their experience, knowledge and skills. The process of actively combating poverty or existing social exclusion is also necessary so that the new arrivals are not used to deprive others of their rights or opportunities in a competitive 'race to the bottom'. Ability and skill should determine their employment, remuneration and conditions of employment, rather than their country of origin. Labour agents and middlemen must be controlled in the labour process and proper regulation and employment standards enforced rigorously to protect the rights of the new arrivals and the existing workforce.

Though the evidence to date is not great in this area, our collective efforts can protect the newer arrivals from degrading exploitation and refuse to allow anyone to undermine the pay rates and conditions of employment, established by us through years of trade union or political effort. Employers need to be made aware of the serious consequences that will flow from opportunist exploitation of migrant workers. It's that profiteering from the vulnerability of migrants which can engender

Organising diversity

bitter resentment and can generate a racist reaction among insecure indigenous workers.

We all remember the Irish Ferries debacle and the huge nationwide resentment it created over the 'displacement' of existing employees. It's also well worth striving to involve the newcomers in their own protection through better-focused organisation and the provision of practical information for those who need it most. The Gamma experience shows the importance of direct communication with migrant workers and the importance of overcoming language difficulties to ensure that they know their rights and can be protected from unfair treatment.

The FÁS 'Know Before You Go' initiative, which provides information in their own languages in their home countries, is a useful example of what can be done. The decision of SIPTU, our largest trade union to employ organisers with Eastern European languages is another good example of adaptation to the new challenge. Likewise many local voluntary groups have been magnificent in their humanitarian and very practical responses to migrants and asylum seekers. Greater access to language teaching is also a vital part of the acceptance process and one that must be greatly expanded in every town and village in Ireland. We should also share with theM a knowledge and appreciation of our Irish language and culture so they can truly feel that they belong. Curiously enough, the Irish language can be one of the unifying elements if approached in a truly open and inclusive way that involves rather than excludes newcomers.

We now have our first Minister of State for Integration. He faces a major challenge, one which we hope he can meet. He has called on the major sporting, business and religious organisations to do more to integrate migrants and we hope this will get the desired response. This would be a welcome development if our efforts to avoid an 'insider-outsider' society are to be successful. These are the initiatives that can become the building blocks of social integration and can cumulatively become, in time, a total Irish openness to the new arrivals. It will not happen automatically, it requires proactive integration measures from government down.

With all this new energy, greater diversity and young blood, I am confident that we will become a better and stronger community. We can seek to weave all the diverse strands into a deeper and richer green tapestry of a pluralist Ireland in which equality and human rights are greatly valued. We did not make a great job of sorting out the Catholic-Protestant conflict on this island over many generations but I hope we are now more mature and understand the importance of dialogue, dignity and mutual respect. Surely some of our petty local squabbles about difference will be more manageable in a context where we will have to accommodate a far greater number of differences on this island.

It is my firm conviction that only by adopting an open and inclusive concept of Irishness can we truly represent both the future and the past of a 'proud people' who are one of the most dispersed and now most diverse peoples of the world. In the end, I place my faith in that 'large and respectable class' of the community, the ordinary decent citizens of Ireland. We can draw inspiration from the

Class of 2007

next generation, with thanks to the teachers who are doing so much to encourage genuine integration and mutual understanding in the classrooms. We need more of them. They deserve our full support and the necessary resources to demonstrate our serious commitment to a real Irish homecoming for all the children of the nation.

A Few New Shades of Green

We live in stirring times. We are probably the first generation in a thousand years with the opportunity, the resources and the people to actually build a new Irish Republic worthy of all the sacrifices, suffering and struggle of previous generations. We can, in this era, actually fulfil Robert Emmett's dream of taking our place among the nations of the earth. We have won the right to live and work at home or to travel and see the world as we see fit. We have a young, bright and vibrant population of all shapes and sizes, optimistic about the future.

There is no need for hunger or homelessness in this country. There is no lack of education or training opportunities and certainly no lack of money, although it's not always available in the places where it is needed most. We have finally achieved an 'historic compromise' in Northern Ireland that offers great promise for the future. Now we face the real task of nation building, of bringing people together in civilised society and shaping our own destiny. It can be as green, as orange or as multi- coloured as we wish to make it. Our children and their children deserve nothing less than the best that we can give them. Given that colour is merely a function of climate, global warming could soon give us all a darker hue.

Pro–Democracy

While new waves of immigration and an increasingly diverse population may present us with certain challenges, we also now have an opportunity for some introspection and self-examination. Rather than viewing newcomers to our shores as 'others' with fundamentally different values, cultures and customs, we should perhaps glance back through our history and ask who exactly are we and what are 'our values'? A cursory look shows that the traditional stereotypes of our national character were never entirely accurate, while the make up of our population has been reshaped and renewed by successive waves of conquest, immigration and emigration.

However, where we came from and what we think we are, are less important than what we want to be. Knowing more about our past does help us to understand the present and the future but we must guard against becoming prisoners of the past.

Yet, by taking a long cold look at who we are, at our successes and our failures, we can more confidently move on. We do have choices to make. What is it from the past that is valuable and worth keeping, what should be discarded and replaced by something better? New people bring new ideas, new opportunities and new cultural influences, just as we have brought our values and our talents to so many parts of the globe.

This generation is very different from any that has gone before, with better opportunities and far more choices about how we live our lives. Yet, we have good reason to be proud of our ancestors, who ever they were, for their indomitable courage in adversity and their sheer determination to survive. They left us an interesting multi-faceted culture, which continues to add a colourful aspect to all our lives. They drew their strength from many different people of all shades and colours. Most of them came here at some time in the past as migrants seeking a safe and secure place to live. They grew in time to love this country and shared with those who went before, or who came after, a remarkable pride of place and a genuine love of their adopted, green and misty, island home. We may now have a few new shades of green, to add to the mind's eye, some darker and some lighter, but then we always had a wonderful tapestry of different colours on the Irish landscape, bringing a soft richness and beauty to all our lives.

Index of Photographs

page 1
'No man has a right to fix the
boundary to the march of a nation'
Charles Stewart Parnell
O'Connell Street, Dublin

page 4-5
'Lively Limerick', enjoying the
festive spirit at the International
BBQ Festival

page 7
'A long way from Molly Malone'.
Today's Moore Street,
Dublin City

page 8
School children
Glebe National School,
Wicklow Town

page 10
Katherine Joyce from the North Island of
New Zealand and her husband Richard, a
landscape designer. Katherine is Maori on
her mother's side with a Scottish father. She
has lived in Ireland since 1990.

page 11
Karleng Chan from Malaysia,
quantity surveyor, collecting
for Cancer on Grafton St. *'I got
bored with shopping and decided to
do charity work instead'.*

122

page 13
Brazilians dancing at the
Quadrilha Festival in Gort,
Co. Galway

page 14-15
Amelia Stein, photographer
Born in Dublin of Jewish parents, she was
the first photographer to be accepted as a full
member of the Royal Hibernian Academy.

page 16-17
'Man of Aran'
Liam O'Flaherty, famous Irish
writer, born on the Aran Islands

page 18
Big Jim Larkin, Irish labour
leader, born in Liverpool, 'The
great only appear great because
we are on our knees'.

page 20
Protestor at the aborted Love
Ulster Parade,
Parnell Street, Dublin City

page 22
Shaqira Hanim and Lisa Desi,
students from Bali, Indonesia at
the festival of World Cultures,
Dunlaoghaire

page 24-25
Traveller couple on the Croagh
Patrick Pilgrimage which is held
on the last Sunday of July every
year, Co. Mayo.

page 20
Children playing in Noah's Ark
at the festival of World Cultures,
Dunlaoghaire

page 22
Joel d'Anjou, guesthouse owner, Inis
Mor, Aran Islands. He has been living
on the Islands for 24 years and is a fluent
Gaelic speaker.

page 30-31
Grace and her sister Susanna came to Ireland
from Ghana in 1993. According to Grace,
(right) 'it's entirely up to any person to adjust
to a new surrounding, one cannot expect
another to make you comfortable as this is
only something you can do, especially when
you come to a new country'.

page 32
Regina O'Connor from Rwanda was married
to an Irishman and came to Ireland in
1986. She was a keen gardener and featured
in Jane Power's column in the Irish Times
in 2003. Her body was found in her house
in Blackrock and a post-mortem confirmed
that she had been murdered.

page 34-35
Three African women on the Kenyan
stand at the International BBQ Festival,
Limerick City

page 36-37
Professor John Jackson, born in Cheltenham,
England. He was the Dean of the Sociology
department in Trinity College, Dublin. He
and his wife adopted two African children
in the 1960's and raised them along with
their two other children.

page 38-39
'A nation on the march'
International celebrations on Saint Patrick's
Day, O'Connell Street, Dublin

page 41
Greg Speranskey, born in Russia and working
now as a grave digger in Glasnevin cemetry

page 42
Bosnian mother and child, Clare Street,
Dublin City. The conflict in the Balkans has
displaced many people .

page 43
Valasi, born in Belarus, came to Ireland as
part of the Chernoble Childrens Project.
When in Ireland he resides with the Starr
family near Balinasloe, Co. Galway.

page 45
'Multi-cultural perspectives'
Spectators watch the Saint Patrick Day
parade on Dublin's O'Connell St.

page 46
Willie Van Velzen, part a dream team of designers from Holland invited here by the Irish Goverment in the 1950's. He has worked extensively with Aer Lingus and his illustrations would be familliar to many Irish people

page 48-49
Killian Schurmann, glass artist, was born to Dutch parents who came to Ireland in the 1950's. His work has been featured in many national and international shows and in the collections of AIB, OPW and the Ulster Museum

page 50-51
Hanne Gillespie is an artist and yoga instructor. Originally from Norway she has lived and worked in Ireland since the late 1970's.

page 53
Marcus Flaherty, Jarvey, born on Inis Mor, Aran Islands. The Aran Islands are now home to 26 different nationalities.

page 54
Afia and Mick Fortune. Afia was born in Ghana and has lived in Ireland for 16 years. Together they run Fortune Plant Hire in Co. Wicklow.

page 56-57
Azad Shirazi, was born in Iran, educated in London and moved to Ireland in 1990. He is now married to an Irish woman and owns a number of successful restaurants and a Persian carpet showroom.

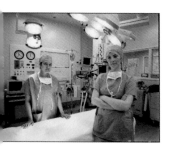

page 58
Sandra Montedonica from Chile and Maria Menezes from Goa, India, Paediatric doctors in the operating theatre of Tallaght Hospital

page 59
Members of the Philipino community participating in the Saint Patrick's Day parade in Bray, Co. Wicklow

page 61
Bruno Palma is from Portugal and has been living in Ireland for three years. He studies animation and works as a part time figure model in the Royal Hibernian Academy.

page 62-63
Rowan Gillespie, one of Ireland's leading sculptors, was born to Irish parents of Quaker stock and grew up in Cyprus. He is best known for a number of prominent works including the Famine monument on Dublin's quays and the Yeats sculpture in Sligo.

page 65
Artist Gerald Davis pictured as Leopold Bloom at the Blomsday celebrations in Dublin. When asked the question 'What is a Nation? Joyce's Bloom replies, 'A nation? ... A nation is the same people living in the same place.'

page 66
Eclectic collection of street signs, Moore St. Dublin City

page 69
Claudio Tamburrini, was born in the Isle of Man and came to Ireland at the age of two where his parents ran Italian restaurants. Now the owner of a thriving motor business specializing in the sale of exotic Italian cars and motorcycles, He feels that 'life is good in Ireland, bar the weather'.

page 70
Sergio Benedetti was born in Florence, Italy. He is Head Curator and Keeper of the Collection of the National Gallery of Ireland. He has resided in Ireland for the past 29 years and is well known for his rediscovery of the Caravaggio masterpiece, The Taking of Christ.

page 71
Vinnie Caprani, Dublin wit, raconteur and writer of Italian extraction. A printer by trade, he has been an active trade unionist all his life and a chronicler of the Italian influence on Irish society. There is a reference to his family in Joyce's Ulysses, 'Caprani too, printer, more Irish than the Irish.'

page 72
Members of the Orange Order on parade

page 73
One of many bands celebrating the 12th of July, Belfast City

page 74
Chinese phone card sellers, Moore St., Dublin City. It is said that there is now more Chinese spoken in Ireland than Gaelic.

page 76
Polish contruction workers enjoying a weekly
soccor match

page 78-79
Three generations of the Moorehouse traveller
family on a slip-road to the N11, Bray, Co.
Wicklow. 'We have it tough living in caravans
at the side of the road, but I feel sorry for the
homeless with no roof to keep out the rain,' -
Mrs Moorehouse senior

page 80
Seán McBride, statesman and former
republican leader, was born in Paris in 1904.
He was the Irish Minister for External
Affairs from 1948-1951 and was a recipient
of both the Nobel Peace Prize and the
Lenin Peace Prize. He was also a barrister
and was one of the founding members of
Amnesty International.

page 82
Nuala ni Dhomhnaill was born in
Lancashire, England of Irish speaking
parents. She has lived in the Dingle
Gaeltacht since 1980 and is the author
of many collections of poetry. She has
been the recipient of numerous awards
including the American Ireland Fund
Literature Prize (1991).

page 84-85
Enkhbaatar Natsagdorj and Tulga
Oyunchimeg are chefs from Mongolia. They
work in a Dublin restaurant and have been saving money to return to their home country to
attend the celebrations marking the 800-year
anniversary of the birth of Ghengis Khan.

page 87
Born in South Africa, Moosajee Bhamjee
came to Ireland in 1965 where he studied
medicine at the college of Surgeons. A former
labour party politician and TD for Clare, he
was elected to the Dáil in November 1992.

page 88
Cousins Nausheen Amhed from Lahore, wife
of the Pakistani Ambassador to Ireland and
Rosheen Callender (nee Yasin) of SIPTU,
long time contributor to national social policy
in Ireland, who was born in Karachi. The two
were recently reunited in Dublin.

page 89
Sahoko Blake was born in Tokyo, Japan and
has been living in Ireland since 1995. She is
an artist and has taken part in many solo and
group exhibitions. She also teaches art and
drawing in her studio and in the NGI and
RHA Galleries.

page 90
Mark Banchansky was born and educated in the
United States. He was introduced to Ireland when he
was offered a contract to work for Aer Rianta, based in
Dublin Airport, overseeing the retail product offering
in Aer Rianta operated duty free shops in Ireland. Six
years later he has no plans to return to the states and his
intention is to remain living and working in Ireland.

page 93
Chinese Falun Gong practitioners stage a peaceful protest against the treatment of fellow practitioners in China, St. Stephen's Green, Dublin

page 94-95
Svetlana Lavery was born in the Ukraine where she worked as a marine Architect. She specialised in the hull design of nuclear submarines in the closed city of Sevastopol on the Black Sea. She has been living in Ireland for 5 years and is currently studying painting and life drawing.

page 96-97
The Palestinian Ambassador to Ireland speaks at a protest to mark the 40th anniversary of the 1967 war and the occupation of Arab lands by Israel

page 96-97
Tanya Kiang was born in London, the daughter of a Chinese father and Swiss mother. She is the director of the Gallery of Photography in Dublin's Temple Bar and has lived in Ireland since she was two years old and considers herself to be very 'Irish.'

page 100-101
Construction workers on the Luas line. Many of the recent major contstruction projects in Ireland were completed with the active involvement of many migrant workers.

page 102-103
Afghans on hunger strike in St. Patrick's Cathedral. The men had refused to leave the cathedral until they were granted asylum.

page 104-105
David Spathaky was born in Portadown, Northern Ireland and now lives in Beara, West Cork. He holds the Guinness world record for simultaneously spinning 108 dinner plates on poles, a record unbroken in 14 years.

page 107
Maja Binder from Germany and Olivier Beaujonan from France. Together they run their organic fine food business from their base on the Dingle Peninsula.

page 108
Nina Kyriakopoulos was born in Germany of Greek parents and came to Ireland sixteen years ago. She is seen here training for currach racing in Dingle Harbour.

page 109
Peter Zoller was born in Germany and has been in Ireland since 1980. He now lives in Tahilla, Co. Kerry and is known for his colourful photographs of the Irish landscape. He is the author of several photographic books.

page 110-111
Phil Lynott was born in England to a Brazilian father and Irish mother. He was the lead singer with the famous Thin Lizzy, whose first hit was 'Whiskey in the Jar.' He took his inspiration from the great Jimmy Hendrix.

page 112
Joe Thoma, artist and musician was born in Scotland to a Polish father and an Irish mother. The family moved to Kenmare in 1959 where his father became the local vet.

page 114
Baya and Nacer Merad from Algeria, with their two children Slami and Roumaissa. They are both GP's and Baya works with the hospice in Harold's Cross and also helped out in the Special Olympics. They have lived in Ireland for four years.

page 115
Abdulsalam Abubaker was born in Somalia. While attending CBS Synge Street he was the winner of the BT Young Scientist of the year 2007 with a project entitled 'An Extension on Wiener's Attack on RSA', which involves a new method of breaking security encryption codes. He recently also claimed a top prize at the EU's Contest for Young Scientists in Valencia, Spain.

page 117
Evelina Sadukyte was born in Lithuania and is currently working for SIPTU's organising unit. Since coming to Ireland she has worked as a childminder and mushroom picker. She speaks fluent Lithuanian, Russian and English and set up a newspaper for Lithuanians in Ireland.

page 119
Students from many different ethnic backgrounds, St. Andrews College, Blackrock, Co. Dublin.

page 121
Chaw-Kalayar was born in Burma and has lived in Co. Sligo for 4 years. She is seen here along with her twin sons setting up for a rally to support demorcracy in Burma.

Bibliography

California Newsreel, (2003) 'Race - the Power of Illusion. Ten Things Everyone Should Know About Race'. www.newsreel.org

Callender, R, (1999) 'Race Discrimination; Where do we stand and what can we do?' Presentation at ICCL Equality Conference, Dublin Castle, 23rd October 1999.

Central Statistics Office, (2006) 'Preliminary Report- Census 2006', The Stationery Office, Dublin.

Clarke, HB (ed), (1995) 'Irish Cities', Mercier Press, Cork.

Cronin, M and Ó Cuilleanáin, C (eds), (2003) 'The Languages of Ireland', Four Courts Press, Dublin.

Dillon-Malone, A, (1996) 'The Guinness Book of Humorous Irish Anecdotes', Guinness Publishing, Middlesex.

Douglass, F, (1995) 'Narrative of the Life of Frederick Douglass', Constable, London.

Douglass, F, (1845) 'I am Here to Spread the Light on American Slavery', an address delivered in Cork, Ireland on 14th October 1845.

Eagleton, T, (1999) 'The Truth About the Irish', St Martin's Press, New York.

European Commission against Racism and Intolerance. (2001) 'Compilation of ECRI's General Policy Recommendations', Council of Europe, Strasbourg.

Fitzgerald, G, (1992) 'Repulsing Racism: Reflections on Racism and the Irish', Attic Press, Dublin.

Foster, RF, (1993) 'Paddy and Mr. Punch: Connections in Irish and English History', The Penguin Press, London.

Geraghty, D and Callender, R, (2000) 'Promoting Diversity and Preventing Racism', Joint Presentation at the ICTU National Conference, 'Ireland: Racist or Multi-Cultural?'

Hardiman, J, (1975) 'A History of the Town and County of Galway' (Originally Published 1820), Kenny's Bookshops and Art Galleries, Galway.

Joyce, J, (2000) 'Ulysses', Penguin Classics, London.

Keogh, D, (1998) 'Jews in Twentieth Century Ireland', Cork University Press, Cork.

La Malfa, C, (2006) 'Italians in Ireland: A Brief History', based on public lecture given by the author on may 1st 2003 at Trinity College Dublin.

Lentin, R and McVeigh, R (eds), (2002) 'Racism and Anti-Racism in Ireland', BTP Publications Ltd., Belfast.

McMahon, S (ed.), (1984) 'A Book of Irish Quotations', The O'Brien Press, Dublin.

Migrant Rights Centre Ireland, (2006) 'Annual Report 2006', MCRI, Dublin.

Migrant Rights Centre Ireland, (2004) 'Private Homes: A Public Concern – The Experiences of Twenty Migrant Women Employed in the Private Home in Ireland', MCRI, Dublin.

Mikhail, EH (ed), (1982) 'Brendan Behan, Interviews and Recollections, Vol. 2', Barnes and Noble Books, New Jersey.

Moloney, M, (2002) 'Far from the Shamrock Shore: The Story of Irish-American Immigration Through Song', The Collins Press, Cork.

National Consultative Committee on Racism and Interculturalism, (2004) 'Progress Report 2002-2004 and Strategy Statement 2005-2007'.

O'Cleary, C, (1986) 'Phrases Make History Here: A Century of Irish Political Quotation', The O'Brien Press, Dublin.

O'Farrell, P, (1994) 'Green and Chaste and Foolish: Irish Literary and Theatrical Anecdotes', Gill and Macmillan, Dublin.

Ó Gráda, C, (2006) 'Jewish Ireland in the Age of Joyce: A Socio-Economic History', Princeton University Press, Oxford.

Oppenheimer, S, (2007) 'The Origins of the British', Constable and Robinson Ltd, London.

Ormsby, F (ed), (1991) 'The Collected Poems of John Hewitt', Blackstaff Press, Belfast.

O'Riordan, M, (2007) 'GAA Founder no Blooming Anti-Semite: Reflections by Manus O'Riordan on some aspects of Irish Jewish history in the age of Joyce', published online at http://www.anfearrua.com

O'Riordan, M, (2005) 'Connelly Column: The Story of the Irishmen who Fought for the Spanish Republic 1936-1939', Warren and Pell, Torfaen.

Rolston, B and Shannon, M, (2002) 'Encounters: How Racism Came to Ireland', BTP Publications, Belfast.

Ruckenstein, L and O'Malley, JA (eds.), (2004) 'Everything Irish: the History, Literature, Art, Music, People and Places of Ireland from A-Z', Mercier Press, Cork.

SIPTU Equality Unit, (2005) 'Organising Diversity: Proceedings of SIPTU's National Women's Forum 2005'.

Spense, J (ed), (1994) 'The Sayings of Jonathan Swift', Gerald Duckworth and Co. Ltd., London.

Sykes, B, (2006) 'Blood of the Isles: Exploring the Genetic Roots of our Tribal History', Bantam Press, London.

Wigham, ML, (1992) 'The Irish Quakers: A Short History of the Religious Society of Friends in Ireland', Historical Society of the Religious Society of Friends in Ireland, Dublin.

Yeats, WB, (1990) 'WB Yeats: Collected Poems', Pan Books Ltd., London.

National Organisations Dealing With Diversity

Association of Refugees and Asylum Seekers in Ireland (ARASI),
213 North Circular Road, Dublin 7, Dublin, Tel: 01- 8381142
Website: www.arasi.org

Comhlamh,
10 Upper Camden Street, Dublin 2 Tel: 01-4783490
Website: www.comhlamh.org

FÁS,
27-33 Upper Baggot Street, Dublin 4 Tel: 01 6070500
Website: www.fas.ie

Immigrant Council of Ireland,
2 St Andrews Lane, Dublin 2 Tel: 01- 6740202
Website: www.immigrantcouncil.ie

Integrating Ireland,
17 Lower Camden Street, Dublin 2, Tel: 01- 4759473
Website: www.integratingireland.ie

Irish Congress of Trade Unions (ICTU),
Parnell St., Dublin 1 Tel: 01-8897777
Website: www.ictu.ie

Irish Refugee Council,
88 Capel Street, Dublin 1 Tel: 01- 873 0042
Website: www.irishrefugeecouncil.ie

Irish Traveller Movement,
4/5 Eustace Street, Dublin 2 Tel: 01- 6796577
Website: www.itmtrav.com

Migrant Rights Centre Ireland,
55 Parnell Square West, Dublin 1 Tel: 01 8897570
Website: www.mrci.ie

NASC Irish Immigrant Support Centre,
St Marie's of the Isle, Sharman Crawford Street, Cork Tel: 0214317411
Website: www.nascireland.org

National Consultative Council on Racism and Interculturalism (NCCRI)
Jervis House, Jervis St., Dublin 1 Tel: 01-8588000
Website: www.nccri.ie

Pavee Point,
46 North Great Charles St, Dublin 1 Tel: 01-8780255
Email: pavee@iol.ie

Refugee Information Service,
27 Annamore Terrace, off North Circular Road, Dublin 7 Tel : 01- 838 2740
Website: www.ris.ie

Services Industrial Professional Technical Union (SIPTU),
Liberty Hall, Dublin 1 Tel: 01-8586300
Website: www.siptu.ie

The Equality Authority,
2 Clonmel Street, Dublin 2 Tel: 01 4173333
Website: www.equality.ie

Cultural Organisations

Africa Centre,
9c Abbey Street Lower, Dublin 1 Tel: 01 8656951
Website: www.africacentre.ie

Brazilian Association of Gort, c/o Gort Family Resource Centre,
Church Street, Gort, Co Galway, Tel: 091 630 902

Diverse Eireann – Diverse Arts and Culture in Ireland,
Unit 2 Mill House, Mill Road, Ennis, Clare, Ireland,
Website: www.diverseeireann.org

Dublin Multicultural Resource Centre, 44 Lower Gardiner Street, Dublin 1,
Tel: 01 8730684   Email: awadmrc@yahoo.com

Irish Speaking Migrants in Ireland and Irish -Speakers of Immigrant Background,
5/609 South Circular Road, Kilmainham, Dublin 8,
Email: imeasc@eircom.net

Islamic Cultural Centre of Ireland,
19 Roebuck Road, Clonskeagh, Dublin 14 Tel: 01- 2080000
Website: www.islamireland.com

Jewish Ireland, Herzog House, 1 Zion Road, Rathgar, Dublin 6
Tel: 01- 4923751 Website: www.jewishireland.com

Latin America Solidarity Centre(LASC), 5 Merrion Row, Dublin 2
Tel: 01-6760435 Website www.lasc.ie

Polish Information and Cultural Centre in Dublin,
56-57 Lower Gardiner Street, Dublin 1, Tel: 01-6729997
Website: www.polishcentre.ie

Sports Against Racism in Ireland,
135 Capel Street, Dublin 1 Tel: 01-8735077 Website www.sari.ie

A complete directory of migrant organisations, including regional, local and community groups, is available on the website of the Immigrant Council of Ireland.